Against All Odds

The Remarkable Life Story of Eddie Ray

Eddie Ray

With Barbara Jackson Hall

Cover Design Concept by Veronica Cordle

ISBN-10: 1478213477
ISBN-13: 9781478213475
Library of Congress Control Number: 2012912483
CreateSpace Independent Publishing Platform
North Charleston, South Carolina

To my children, Eddie, Jr., Donald, Teresa, and Michael, who have brought so much joy and inspiration into my life. Also to my wife, Jeanette, for her special support throughout the writing of this book. ❧

Prologue

October 3, 2009. I smiled as I looked into the faces of the crowd, 150 guests, all of them dressed in semiformal attire with sequence scattered here and there. It was an occasion of a lifetime, at least my lifetime. I was being inducted into the new North Carolina Music Hall of Fame.

I had received some two hundred awards and honors throughout my sixty-year-career in the commercial music business, but this particular occasion brought somewhat of an epiphany for me. Of course I was humbled by the prestigious honor, but the truth is, what also gave me pause was the actual physical venue for the event. It was, for lack of a better term, odd.

The building was elegant all right, with white Italian marble floors that extended halfway up the walls. Gold-plated elevators. A huge hand-carved oak table in the lobby. But this location was far from a big city, fancy hotel where these types of highbrow events usually occur. Upstairs was a research laboratory of all things, actually several laboratories—research with mice, DNA, and petri dishes.

This auspicious occasion was being held in the David H. Murdock Core Laboratory, opened by the Dole Foods magnate only a year prior in Kannapolis, North Carolina. Why was this event being held here? That's the odd part.

As I stood in the lobby of this research facility, looking at familiar faces from my past and present, I thought, *After traveling the world, how in the world did I wind up back in rural North Carolina?* Yes. It was par for the course. An odd venue symbolic of a life filled with me landing in unlikely places.

CHAPTER ONE

TAPESTRY

Let me say this at the outset. I don't sing or dance. I don't play an instrument or read music. So the next question I'm usually asked is, "Well, how in the world did you stay in the record business for sixty years?" I'm ready for that one.

"I have no idea," I quickly respond with a bemused expression, knowing I'm about to see the wheels of curiosity turning as the questioner tries to figure out whether I'm serious or being facetious. Then with a light tap on their arm and whatever sincerity I can muster, I add, "Strange, isn't it? Certainly against all odds, don't you think?" They pause, slowly nod, and from there the conversation takes any number of enjoyable directions.

The truth is I do know the answer to my longevity in the music industry, but since it takes a book like this to explain, "I have no idea" works so much better on the spur of the moment.

The answer is that I've been blessed with two gifts. First, I have the ability to recognize talent early on in others. As one acquaintance put it recently when recalling my success, she said I "had an ear for what would sell." The second gift is I have an innate sense of timing, not rhythm, but timing; it's like the lyrics to the song "The Gambler" by Kenny Rogers. I have a sense of knowing when to "hold 'em, fold 'em, walk away, or run." Take those two gifts and wrap them in enough courage to bend the rules, and you have my formula for success.

I've thought a lot about the best way to capture my life's story, and the image that keeps forming is that of a tapestry where people—vivid, bold, or not so bright, even muted—people are threads woven through events to create this colorful, seamless work that's stretched out over a loom spanning six decades. That's what I see and what I want readers to picture in these pages.

Some names will be immediately recognized, especially by baby boomers. Some threads in the tapestry are strong and long—people appearing and reappearing throughout most of my career. Others are short threads, but very thick, those who have had a brief, yet powerful impact on my life. But all of the people I encountered along the way are still very important to me, even though many, if not most, are no longer living.

⁓

I arrived in Los Angeles, California, two days before Thanksgiving in 1945 with no job, no money, and no place to stay. I had just come in by train from Milwaukee, where I'd spent the previous four months. Milwaukee was an interesting experience for this eighteen-year-old. Actually it was where I got my first job at a record company, so I guess you could say it was the beginning of my career in the business. Articles about me usually start in Milwaukee, with a headline like "From Stock Boy to Top Record Industry Executive." Milwaukee was the stock boy part.

All I saw when I arrived in the industrialized Wisconsin city that summer were these big smoke stacks from foundries making iron and steel castings for war equipment and, sure enough, that's where the employment agency first sent me. I walked into one of the foundries and looked around at the hot, noisy, dangerous environment. I saw these huge six-foot-five, over 200-pound guys hoisting molten metal, pouring it into a mold. There I was, a five-foot-something teen, with an average weight of 130 pounds at most. The guys took one look at me and yelled, "Get out of here. There's no way you're going to handle this kind of job!" They got no argument from me. I went back to the employment agency.

"Well, I see here we have a job listed where you can work as a stock boy at a record distributing company called Decca Records on Clyborne Street."

"I'll take it."

I didn't know anything about Decca at the time but soon found out that the record company dated back to the late 1920s, when former stockbroker Edward Lewis bought it from The Decca Gramophone Company and within a few years turned it into a huge record label. Where I worked in Milwaukee was only one of about twenty-five or thirty Decca wholesale distributors in the country. Artists with Decca in the 1930s and '40s included Louis Armstrong, Count Basie, The Boswell Sisters, Billie Holiday, The Andrews Sisters, Judy Garland, The Mills

Brothers, Guy Lombardo, The Ink Spots, Dorsey Brothers, and many more.

In fact one of my memorable experiences as a stock boy at Decca was when I began to notice we were shipping a lot of boxes with the same code number. *What is this record that's selling so well?* My curiosity was piqued. I found out that it was "White Christmas" by Bing Crosby, another Decca artist, the first year it was released as a single record. It had previously been released as part of a movie soundtrack album. To me it's rather interesting that long before I even thought about a career in record sales and promotion, the timing of my very first record industry job exposed me to the sales of one of the greatest hit records of all time.

But there's an even more memorable coincidence about Milwaukee. On my way to work at Decca each day, I would pass a beautiful hotel downtown, right where I changed busses. I'd see people in limos and big fancy cars going in and out of there. *One day I'm going in that hotel*, I told myself and eventually did to see what it was like. *I'll just get a cup of coffee.* I stepped into the hotel, and it was as beautiful as I imagined, with marble floors, expensive antiques, ornate chandeliers, and imported rugs.

After being duly impressed, I headed for the coffee shop and couldn't believe how expensive everything was—a whopping thirty-five cents for a cup of coffee and thirty cents for a sweet roll. Now, sixty-five cents took a big chunk out of my thirty-dollar-a-week-check, especially since I was used to getting both coffee and a Danish for around twenty cents from the vending trucks that would stop by work.

But the interesting part about this hotel was that just eleven years later I was a guest there, staying in a huge suite, on the top floor. I was the national record promotions/sales manager for the number one recording artist for that year—Ricky Nelson. Actually we had the entire floor. As I sat back in my suite that time, I said to myself, *Mama, I wish you could see me now.*

The weeks passed quickly at Decca, and as the summer ended, the weather began to turn cold. I knew Milwaukee winters could be brutal, and that wasn't going to work for a young man born and raised in the mild climate of North Carolina. All it took for me to turn my sights toward warmer weather was to see an ad in a travel magazine depicting the beauty of sunny California. *That's where I need to be.* So one cold November morning I took my meager savings, boarded a train, and headed for sunnier skies. On the train, I asked one of the black porters if he knew of a good, cheap room that I could rent once in Los Angeles.

"Most of us stay in a hotel on Fifth Street, and I think they rent rooms by the week," he replied.

I made my way to Fifth Street, not expecting anything very nice, and I was right. I was not only disappointed but shocked at the condition of the hotel and the street—known as a hangout for bums, winos, and degenerates of all kinds, but I didn't have an option.

On December 21, 1945, I celebrated my nineteenth birthday in that skid-row hotel room, broke and alone with only a dream that California was where I needed to be. I took odd jobs through an employment agency, including washing dishes in a seafood restaurant and pots in the kitchen of a Hollywood hospital, determined to move from Fifth Street as soon as possible.

Even though I had made impulsive and sometimes irrational decisions in my life up until that point, I knew one of the best decisions I could make was to continue my education, so I enrolled in Los Angeles City College to pursue a degree in business administration.

Then an employment break happened in the summer of 1946. The employment agency told me about a job in the shipping department at Aladdin Records. Since I had already worked as a stock boy at Decca, I knew the job would be a good fit. A great coincidence was that Aladdin was only a few blocks from LACC, where I had planned to start classes that fall.

Aladdin was owned by two Lebanese brothers, Leo and Eddie Mesner, and it was one of a rapidly growing number of record manufacturing companies that sprang up right after World War II. Prior to 1945 practically all of the commercially recorded music in America was manufactured or produced and distributed by four major record companies—RCA, Columbia Records, Decca, and Capitol Records.

But after the war, the industry went through a major transition. Smaller record companies, known as "independents," started forming, some as record manufacturers and others as independently owned record distributors. The independent manufacturers would sign an artist, produce the record, and put it on the company label. Then they outsourced the distribution and sales of the record to the independent record distribution companies, unlike the major companies that owned their own distribution outlets.

The independents developed a successful network of record production and distribution all over the country that bypassed the tightly controlled, conservative, elitist major companies. The four major companies also had limited the recordings of African Americans primarily to popular big bands like Duke Ellington, Lionel Hampton, and Count Basie or singers such as Ella Fitzgerald, Nat King Cole, Dinah Washington, and Lena Horne. The Ink Spots and Mills Brothers and other established groups were also on major labels during that time. But those big-named artists were just the tip of the iceberg.

What the independents did was open up opportunities for thousands of new musicians, vocalists, and songwriters of every music genre, and the biggest beneficiaries were African Americans, teenagers, and country and gospel artists.

The independents, which eventually numbered around seven hundred, had their own hierarchy with a relatively select few being known as "major independent" record manufacturing or distribution companies. Aladdin was one of the early major independents, along with Atlantic, Mercury, Imperial, Chess, King, and several others. In later years, included among the major independents were three owned or operated by African Americans—Motown, VeeJay, and Duke/Peacock.

Leo and Eddie Mesner had recently formed Aladdin when I joined the company. They had owned a record store in Los Angeles called the Philharmonic Music Shop, and they had first named the company Philo after the shop. When the name was changed, they kept the Philo label to release live concerts by some of their jazz artists when they played at the Philharmonic Music Hall. Providence must have been at work because I couldn't have come by a better opportunity than to encounter the Mesner brothers.

No one would have believed they were brothers. They didn't favor each other, and their personalities were almost opposite. Leo ran the business side of the company, a Wall Street type with a polished look and conservative suits. Eddie handled the creative side. He was head of A & R (artists and repertoire) and was more of a casual, yet snappy, flashy dresser. He was unconventional, a white man married to a black woman, and drove fancy convertibles. Where Leo may have never ventured to "the other side of the tracks," Eddie practically lived there. But as different as the brothers were, they both took an immediate interest in me.

Leo happened to be a former college professor and continually encouraged me in my studies at LACC.

"How are your classes going? How did you do on that exam?" he would often ask, and sometimes he assisted me with class assignments. He even urged me to take time from work to do homework. He wanted to make sure I continued my education.

Eddie, on the other hand, encouraged me in the creative side of the business. When I began to inquire about the records we were shipping, who the artists were, and how the sales were going, he started bringing artists by and introducing them to me. Since I was only a young shipping clerk, I didn't have much interaction with them other than, "Hello. It's nice to meet you." I just admired them from afar.

One of Aladdin's artists that I met was Charles Brown. I was quite impressed with him probably because I learned he had a bachelor's degree in chemistry and worked as a schoolteacher and chemist before embarking on a music career. Brown had some huge hits with Aladdin such as "Trouble Blues" and "Black Night," which topped the R & B charts for multiple weeks. He was known for his mellow style, sometimes referred to as "nightclub blues." Brown also became known for his popular holiday classics "Merry Christmas Baby" and "Please Come Home for Christmas." During the late '40s and early '50s, he was considered by many to be the most popular blues singer of the day.

I was also introduced to Amos Milburn, another popular Aladdin R & B artist. Milburn, born in Texas, was one of thirteen children and was playing the piano by the age of five. He was with Aladdin for eight years and "Chicken Shack Boogie" was one of his biggest hits with the label. I can still hear the lyrics, *"Hello everybody, this cat is back, looking for a place called the Chicken Shack."*

Mesner would sometimes give me tickets to see Brown, Milburn, or some of their other R & B artists, such as The Five Keys, when they performed at popular black clubs on Central Avenue in Los Angeles's Watts area. He even invited me to concerts with him at the Philharmonic Music Hall to see some of their jazz artists like the Nat King Cole Trio, Billie Holiday, Illinois Jacquet, and Lester Young.

"Would you like to go to a recording session?" Eddie Mesner asked me one day. This gave me my first up-close exposure to the production of a record. I'd go to sessions every chance I could get, sit quietly, and soak up the education. I paid close attention to the overall sound of the music and background vocals and how the recording engineer was able to separate and balance the music and vocal tracts when there were so many people playing and singing at the same time in the tiny studio. I listened to the conversations between Eddie and the engineer.

"Please increase the bass drum," he'd say, or "Could you lower the sound of the background singers? They're covering up the artist's vocals." I'd watch the arranger, Maxwell Davis, a talented African-American musician who was associated with the early hits on the Aladdin label.

At Aladdin I learned about each step in the process from recording a song to it being shipped all over the country. It was during my three years at Aladdin that a spark was ignited for me to consider a career in the music industry, but I didn't know it at the time. I was majoring in business administration at LACC and intended to become a CPA. What did stick with me from the Lebanese brothers, and stayed with me the rest of my life, was the importance of being a mentor.

Leo and Eddie Mesner were among the short, thick treads in the tapestry, people who had a powerful impact on my life. Sadly, I never had a chance to tell them just how important they were in setting the stage for my lifelong career.

CHAPTER TWO

WANDERING NO MORE

P rovidence was at work again in my life. That's the only way I can explain how at nineteen years old I became connected to a church/community center congregation that became so important to me that I stayed with the organization for some eighteen years.

I don't consider myself a religious man, not in the sense of going to church every Sunday listening to denomination dogma about heaven and hell. However the Christian principle of living a life of service was always attractive to me and was an underlying constraining force.

After experiencing the seedy side of Los Angeles on Fifth Street, I was able to scrape up enough money to rent a room on Thirty-Second Street on the east side, however, I didn't spend much time there. I'd leave early to go to work, then directly to school and arrive back around ten or eleven at night. This was every day except the weekends. Occasionally my landlady, Mrs. Smith, would look out for me with a plate of food, which I greatly appreciated. One day we struck up more than a passing conversation.

"I had a friend whose child was involved in a community center program." She continued, "My friend recently invited me to a game to see her kid play and then to the Sunday service of the church that ran the community center." Then the Providential part. With a persuasive tone she said, "I think this is the type of thing you'd like." She added, "I'm not interested in going, but there are a lot of young people there, and I think you might enjoy it." So for reasons I can't explain, I went to the church on East Twentieth Street called All Peoples Christian Church and Community Center, a Disciples of Christ denomination.

Mrs. Smith was right. There were a lot of young people, and what I found unusual was that the church was integrated—Asians, Hispanics, Caucasians, and African Americans all worshipping together. It was probably the only integrated congregation of its kind in Los Angeles at the time.

I signed the guest book, and the very next week, the young Caucasian minister, Dan Genung, came by to visit me. He talked about the different activities of the community center and the groups I could join. He never mentioned the worship service. The next weekend a young lady called saying the center was having a beach party and wondered if they could come by and pick me up. "OK," I replied.

I had a great time at the beach party, and afterward we went to a worship service—in beach clothes. I liked the casual, non-tie wearing, relaxed atmosphere of the church service and the message I heard. The people also fascinated me, some of whom had been in Japanese internment camps. The camps, or "relocation centers" as they were called, were set up soon after the start of World War II. In 1942 President Franklin Roosevelt signed an executive order to round up over one hundred thousand Americans of Japanese descent and send them to one of ten internment camps located in Arizona, Wyoming, Colorado, Arkansas, California, Idaho, and Utah. The reason was the growing anti-Japanese sentiment fueled by the attack on Pearl Harbor.

Fumi Ide, one of those interned, became a good friend of mine at All Peoples. She saved most of the letters other internees had written to her in 1942 and 1943. In later years she compiled the letters and other documents and donated the collection to the Japanese American National History Museum. A few years ago, Ide sent me a sample of the collection, where her friends described loneliness, severe cold, food shortages, and being herded around like cattle. It took me back to those days when I listened intently to the stories of church members.

All Peoples Christian Church and Community Center happened at a crucial point in my young life. It was subconscious at the time, but looking back on it now I realize I was searching for three things.

When I arrived in California in 1945, I was beginning to see myself as a wanderer. I had been away from home for three years, living in different cities, working at odd jobs, even doing a stint in the military. So I needed a foundation, some stability.

I also wanted a social outlet, and it had to be "wholesome." I was never into the drug and alcohol scene, which surprised a lot of people who thought it was so pervasive in the music industry. Despite the media stereotypes, not everyone in the business lives a degenerate lifestyle. I must add, however, that in my opinion the music business does have a way of swallowing up its young. Fans will make a person rich and famous, but the industry will exact a high price, more than a pound of flesh. The performance schedule, the pressure to come out with new material, the loss of a private life to the point of isolation all can force many young stars to seek all sorts of coping mechanisms.

My third quest was to find a way to help others. Again, it wasn't conscious, but even as a young man I knew I was most fulfilled not by being up front but being behind the scenes, doing something for someone else. Through the years, I've found that when you focus on making others successful, success on some level lands on your shoulders. So this particular church offered me everything I needed at the time.

The congregation wasn't huge, about two hundred, so we were like a family, but at the community center we served hundreds of people, especially young people, many from disadvantaged families. We held classes for pregnant teens, had a sports program, fed and clothed young and old, and sponsored a host of other community activities.

I became part of the summer and winter camp program where we would take young people, many of whom had never been off the streets of Los Angeles, up to the mountains above Palm Springs or Big Bear for hiking and horseback riding. Merchants donated goods for fundraisers and even provided vehicles to support the camp program.

All Peoples is where I came alive. I found my social and service niche and was proud to be part of an organization that was accomplishing so much. I became a church elder and the youngest chairman of the board at twenty-one.

I often think about the loving, caring All Peoples family—the Genungs; the Kodamas; the Ides; the Stewards; the Smiths; the Kokubuns; the Mosleys; the Wongs; the Tolberts; the Jordans; the Minors; the Kims; the Inouyes; the Carlocks;

the Gutierrezes; the Hills; the Suzukis; and the many other members. I see them as long, strong threads in the tapestry that will forever be an integral part of me.

With my new job at Aladdin Records and my connection to All Peoples, my professional and social life was on the upswing, and as a matter of fact, so was my personal life.

~~~

"I know you." I ran into her between classes one evening at LACC. She was saying she recognized me from somewhere.

"I know you," she repeated.

"You do?"

"Yes. You used to live next door to my family on Stanford Avenue near Thirty-Third Street."

I had lived there briefly prior to renting from Mrs. Smith and recalled a house with a lot of kids next door. I'd see them coming and going, ranging in age from around five to twenty. I hadn't noticed this brown-skinned beauty then, but I certainly did this day. She introduced herself as Tessie.

Tessie and I became good friends and started dating. Thinking back now, I laugh, saying it must have been my charm that won her because I didn't even have a car, so on dates we'd have to take the streetcar. But she was willing to go anywhere with me.

We were married in the spring of 1947 at LA City Hall and eventually started a family. Her large family wrapped their arms around me like a natural-born son, which I relished since I had been away from home for so long. Tessie also became fairly active at All Peoples, especially in the summer when she would accompany me on recreational outings or volunteer as an instructor in the arts and crafts sessions for the campers.

One day Bob Kodama, a friend at All Peoples, mentioned that I might be interested in going into real estate once I graduated from Los Angeles City College. He said it would mean more money than what I was making at Aladdin. He soon introduced me to the Japanese owner of a local real estate company. So right after I graduated with my associate's degree in business administration, I quit my shipping clerk job at Aladdin and decided to sell real estate at Kashu Realty. I did very well listing properties and at the time thought, *Yes, this is something I'd like to do.* However, after about a year I heard there was an opening at a new record distributing company where I could use the experience I had already gained, so I went for it. Despite the lucrative opportunity in real estate, the record business always pulled at me. I think what I liked most was the creative side, the potential to eventually work with artists in creating hit songs, something that stuck with me watching musicians and singers at work in the small studio at Aladdin Records.

I went to work for Central Record Sales Company in 1950 and never looked back.

CHAPTER THREE

NOT TO BE PIGEONHOLED

The man breezed into the door of Central Record Sales Company and headed in my direction.

"Let me see your boss. I want to talk to your boss," he demanded. But before I could open my mouth, he assumed my skin color meant I had little knowledge and zero authority, so he immediately turned to the white woman a few feet from me.

"Let me see your boss," he continued.

"Well," she said and paused, lifting her eyebrows as if in thought, just to add a little drama. "There he is right there," she replied, motioning to me.

With a look of surprise and a hint of distain, the red-faced man started back in my direction. This time before he could open his mouth, I said, "Whatever you're selling, we don't want any," and dismissed him on the spot.

The year was 1953, and I had been at Central Record Sales Company for three years. I had no time or patience for the foolishness of racism. Of course it was and still is a fact of life for people of color, especially African Americans, so my experiences through the years of being deliberately overlooked, flat out denied, or openly ridiculed were in no way unique.

I will say that because African-American artists were becoming more visible in the music business in the 1950s, I felt I'd at least stand a chance of moving through the ranks of the industry. So I made it a point, actually a personal mission, to break through as many racial barriers as possible. My quest or refusal to be pigeonholed began in earnest when I joined Central Record Sales Company, and my courage for hitting racism head-on matured.

In the hierarchy of independent record distributors, Central Record Sales was in the "major" category. It was the wholesale distributor that handled the sales on the West Coast, primarily Southern California, for just about all of the major independent record manufacturers in the country. I started in a position much higher than my previous record industry jobs. This time I was in charge of the shipping and receiving department and inventory control, supervising a shipping clerk, stock boy, telephone operator, and an inside sales person. I was totally responsible for all inside record sales to the smaller retail stores and jukebox operators who were not serviced by our outside salespersons. These smaller stores had to come to us to make their purchases.

Central's owner was Jim Warren, a very likable young man in his late twenties. I never knew how he was financially able to start an operation like Central at such a young age. However, there were industry rumors that Art Rupp, owner of Specialty Records, a major independent record manufacturer, was Jim's silent financial partner.

Warren was an excellent salesman and primarily serviced all the record outlets in the major department stores like Sears and J.C. Penney along with the largest retail record store in the area, Music City, located on Sunset Boulevard in Hollywood. He was also the record buyer for the company and handled all the business and accounting operations.

During the early 1950s, retail record stores were popping up everywhere around the country in both black and white communities, and it was Central Record's job to get as many of our products in those stores and in jukeboxes in Southern California as possible.

In addition to Warren, the company had three white salesmen who would call on the larger white record stores to push our product, and these stores would generally purchase records by only the white artists we represented. But most black stores, smaller white stores, and jukebox owners had to come to the company or one of the large "One Stops," like California Music, to purchase and pick up their records.

One Stops were subwholesale distributors that purchased records wholesale from both the major and independent record distributors and resold them to smaller retail stores and jukebox operators. One Stops were more convenient for smaller stores and jukebox operators because they were able to purchase all the product they needed from only one location.

Very often some white owner of a small record store would come to Central looking for a particular record that he had begun getting requests for. After learning that we had the record, I would hear racist remarks like, "So you're the guys who sell those records to steal hubcaps by," referring to our black artists.

"Well, for the measly five or six records you're planning to buy, you can keep your money," I'd shoot back. I didn't play.

We had quite a bit of traffic in and out of our doors at Central Record Sales, some of it welcomed, some not, but all of it kept us quite busy.

Being in charge of inventory presented another kind of challenge for me but one that I soon turned into a career opportunity. We had thousands upon thousands of records in stock, and it was my job to know exactly how many records of each song we had. Jim Warren would ask, "Eddie, I'm going to place an order. How many of this particular record title do we have left?" Always having a ready answer meant I had to come in on the weekends or stay late to count each and every record by hand. Thinking back on it now, I just can't imagine how we got along without computers, but we did.

My career opportunity came when one day I approached Warren. "Instead of you placing the orders, Jim, why don't you let me do it? Since I'm the one who knows what we have in stock and am more aware of the current sales demand for a particular record, I can place the orders as needed and relieve you of that task." Warren readily agreed. Asking for more work was one of the career strategies that endeared me to my supervisors and propelled me into management rolls rather quickly throughout my career.

So instead of me telling Jim Warren what we needed, I'd pick up the phone and call a major independent record manufacturer in New York like Atlantic Records or Chess Records in Chicago and say, "I want five thousand of this song or two thousand of that." It meant a new title for me, chief buyer, and a salary increase. It also put me on the radar of most of the big independent record companies in the US and made me the first African American at any record distributor in the country to have such a role. I built strong relationships with record manufacturing companies as well as with the black and white store owners, One Stops, and jukebox owners who came into Central Records to purchase their records.

Anyone who had worked in the record industry for at least one day during that time should have realized the best way to sell a record was for it to get played on the radio. But very few independent record companies had a national radio promotion manager, and none had regional promotion representatives. Instead, the independent record companies depended upon their distributors for radio promotion, who would simply mail promotional records to radio stations, hoping the record would be played. Knowing this, I approached Warren with another idea.

"Jim, how about if I start taking some of our new artists to radio stations to get DJs to play them," I offered. "I will initially work more closely with our major black radio stations, also popular DJs like Hunter Hancock, Dick 'Huggy Boy' Hugg, Art Leboe, and John Dolphin. Then I'll start cultivating the major white pop and top forty radio stations, getting them to play our popular R & B artists." By this time, there wasn't anything Jim wouldn't let me do, because I had already had success with my other major responsibilities.

So when our record manufacturers would call and say, "Eddie, I have five new releases coming out next month, and I'm sending you demos of each," I'd listen to each demo and first decide if I could successfully get it played on at least one of our major radio stations and then decide how many records I could realistically sell. For example, if I thought the record release had a commercial sound like "Sh-Boom" by the Chordcats, I would order several thousand copies. I would then take my promo copies to every radio station in Los Angeles and say,

"You've got to hear this new record. It's going to be a smash hit."

In those days most of the major DJs had free reign over what they would play and would often start playing the record immediately during my visit. Incidentally, "Sh-Boom" by the Chordcats, a black R & B group, was a huge number one R & B and pop hit in the Los Angeles market, while the cover record by the white group, The Crew Cuts, was the number one pop record in the rest of the country.

As time passed I came up with another strategy that not only worked very well in getting my records played and sold but actually solidified my reputation as a true "record man." Since there were several wholesale record distributors in our area representing hundreds of different record companies and retailers, and DJs had difficulty finding out which distributor had a specific artist or song title, with Warren's approval, I compiled a monthly list of all the top selling independent record company artists in the Southern California area, even listing titles from our competitor distributors.

I would state, "This song is going to be a hit, but you have to get it from Record Merchandising Distributor," or "You have to get this from King Distributing Company." I would take maybe five from a competitor, but twenty-five of mine. DJs and retailers began to see me as a trusted resource, not just a salesman. This same strategy worked years later when I promoted for a national record manufacturer. I'd walk into a station and say of my competitor's record, "Have you heard this record on Atlantic Records?" "Have you heard this on RCA? You've got to hear it." Because I became an ally, my records were played.

My sales strategy also helped in my sales to jukebox owners who would come in to Central Records to make purchases. "I have three hundred jukeboxes. I want ten of these country songs for seventy-five boxes and this many R & B songs for another hundred boxes," they'd say. Since I knew what was starting to sell, I could make some solid recommendations that they trusted. I also discovered that with jukebox owners, if they purchased eighteen different records for all of their boxes, for instance, and only three or four of them were hits, they were very happy. "Boy, Eddie, you really know how to pick hits," they'd say of the hit records. They weren't concerned at all about the others that didn't do anything. I was able to get a lot of records into jukeboxes.

My selling success at Central Record Sales Company gave me the confidence to bend the unwritten racial rules. Again, I refused to be pigeonholed or abide by the "white salespeople are to sell to white outlets and black salespeople to black establishments" norm. I would take my promotional records to both R & B and white radio stations, white retail stores and jukebox operators, and the largest white-owned One Stop on the West Coast, California Music.

Looking back at it now, while at Central Record Sales, I promoted and sold the records of a who's who of R & B, gospel, and jazz artists, contributing to their popularity—artists such as B.B. King, who became known for his guitar work in the 1950s; Joe Turner, called "Boss of the Blues," was among the first to mix R & B with boogie-woogie, resulting in what was called "jump blues," a style that preceded rock and roll. His original recording of "Shake, Rattle, and Roll," cut for Atlantic Record in 1954, remains one of the cornerstones of the rock and roll revolution; Ruth Brown may not be a household name today, but her recordings of "Teardrops in My Eyes" and "Mama He Treats Your Daughter Mean" dominated the R & B charts in the 1950s. She, too, was a hit maker for Atlantic Records; Sam Cooke was part of a premier gospel group in the

1950s called The Soul Stirrers before turning to pop music in 1957 with his hit "You Send Me;" Ray Charles's recording of "I've Got a Woman" reached number one on the R & B charts in the mid-1950s and spawned a new genre later to become known as soul, a blend of gospel, blues, and jazz; Roy Hamilton's first big hit was his version of "You'll Never Walk Alone" in 1954; The Orioles, known as the first R & B vocal group, set the pattern for the doo-wop sound and began to make a name for themselves with performances at Harlem's Apollo Theater from 1948 to 1954; The Drifters linked the '50s rhythm and blues with the '60s soul music. Their hits included "There Goes My Baby," "Save the Last Dance for Me," and "This Magic Moment." Also on my Central Records promotion list were gospel artists such as Mahalia Jackson, The Soul Stirrers, The Pilgrim Travelers, and The Roberta Martin Singers, as well as jazz artists James Moody, Sonny Stitt, Lester Young, Stan Getz, King Pleasure, George Shearing, and Illinois Jacquet. The artists I mentioned are just a sample of the talent that made the 1950s such a great music era and certainly not a complete list of the records I handled. But they and many others made a significant contribution to the evolution of today's music.

Since I broke the "white salespeople to white and black salespeople to black outlets" rule, I believe I was responsible for the "crossover market" success of Central Record Sales. However, I always maintained my strong relationships with African-American DJs and store owners. One owner in particular I'll never forget was John Dolphin, owner of Dolphin's of Hollywood Record Shop.

CHAPTER FOUR

A Big Man with Big Talk

A round ten thirty on a Saturday night, the phone rang at home.

"Hi, Eddie, Baby. Business is really jumpin' tonight, and we're selling thousands of your records and—"

"Yeah, John Dolphin," I interrupted. "What do you want? I'm not going to Central Records for any records for you tonight."

"Come on, Baby. It's the first of the month, and people are coming in with their welfare checks and buying records like crazy. Your record by Ruth Brown, 'Mama He Treats Your Daughter Mean,' is a monster hit, and I've got only ten copies left for the entire weekend, and I need at least a thousand more—"

I interrupted again. "John, when you were ordering your records Thursday, I pleaded with you to order more of this hit, so now, good night."

Before I could hang up, he began yelling in the phone. "No, Baby! No, please, just this one last time!"

I acquiesced and with a sigh, calmly asked, "How many records do you want to order tonight, John?"

I could hear the sound of relief in his voice as he replied, "I need a lot of Ruth Brown's 'Mama' hit and some gospel records by Mahalia Jackson, The Soul Stirrers, and that new hit by The Clovers. The total will be about three thousand records. Before I could respond, John added, "Baby, do you know that pretty new sales girl, Laverne, I recently hired? I'll send her over to pick you up and take you to Central for the order." He continued, "I think she has eyes for you, because she asked me who that handsome little guy was with me the other day. She doesn't have to rush back to the store, so you guys can take your time and maybe stop somewhere for a cocktail or something."

I rolled my eyes thinking, *Here we go again.* "John," I cut in with frustration, "I'm not interested in your bull. The most important thing to me is, will you have the cash to pay for your order upon delivery?"

"I promise. I cross my heart to God," he said.

"You've promised before and it was four days before I got the money."

"Baby, that happened only one time when my car broke down on my way to pay you and—"

"Yeah, John, surely you don't expect me to believe that lie. I'll do it this time, but this is the last time."

On my way to Central Records to get his order, I turned on the *John Dolphin Radio Show* and heard him on the air screaming, "The next record, 'Mama He Treats Your Daughter Mean,' by Ruth Brown, is dedicated to my friend and the greatest record man in the world, Mr. Eddie Ray."

Thus describes a typical John Dolphin encounter. However, he was my best retail sales account during my years at Central Record Sales Company. While other record store owners might have purchased dozens of records at a time from me, Dolphin would buy them by the thousands. So whenever he called, whether Thanksgiving, Christmas, or on weekends, I would go, often reluctantly, and unlock Central Records, pick up his order, and deliver it to him.

Dolphin owned four or five record stores in South Central Los Angeles and on the eastside of the city, in predominately African-American and Mexican-American neighborhoods, but his major store, his headquarters, was Dolphin's of Hollywood at Central and Vernon, right in the heart of the inner city. It was open twenty-four hours a day, a popular hangout for independent record promotion and sales personnel and especially for "wanna-be recording artists" hoping to be discovered by some big shot promoter who happened by.

The main attraction was his live radio show, broadcast from the front window that often drew huge sidewalk crowds, especially when some major recording artist was being interviewed. The show was on practically all night playing rhythm and blues from about 9:00 p.m. to 4:00 a.m., followed by two or more hours of black gospel. The live show was a brilliant idea by Dolphin, an excellent way to sell records and promote new artists.

Many of those new artists were produced by Dolphin himself. That was his other business, in addition to owning popular record stores. He was a record producer and promoter and one of the early African-American independent record label owners. He created four labels—Recorded in Hollywood, started in 1950, followed by Lucky. He then formed a label called Money and later the label Cash. Some of his records made the national charts in the 1950s, the biggest being "Jivin' Around" by Ernie Freeman, but most were popular just on the West Coast.

Dolphin obviously used his live radio show to introduce and promote his own artists, but he also put many others on the map in Southern California early in their career; now-famous artists such as Sam Cooke with his song "You Send Me," Ruth Brown's, "Mama He Treats Your Daughter Mean," and Ray Charles who came to California from Seattle, Washington, in the 1950s with his group the Maxim Trio, who recorded on Swing Time Records, another label owned by an African American, Jack Lauderdale. Dolphin sold hundreds of thousands of their records in his stores. In my opinion, he was the most important person in the music business in promoting and selling R & B music in California.

Another one of his successful business ideas was to hire the popular white disc jockey Dick "Huggy Boy" Hugg, who attracted white teens to the store and made an impact on the crossover market. Hugg is credited with breaking the song "Earth Angel" by The Penguins on his show at Dolphin's.

A *character* is probably too mild of a description for John Dolphin. He was a boisterous guy who would take command of any conversation. I've seen him described as a "big man with a big cigar, big talk, and big promises," which was pretty accurate. The words *hustler* and *con man* were always somewhere in the description as he was often accused of leaving his artists standing at the cash register.

Dolphin weighed maybe 250 pounds, was well dressed, always in a suit and tie with matching socks, shoes, and hat. He purchased most of his expensive, tailor-made suits from Sy Devore, the popular Hollywood and Beverly Hills stores where the top actors and producers shopped.

The only person I knew who could commandeer his big personality, literally shut him down on the spot, was his lovely, mild-mannered, petite wife, Ruth.

"Eddie, Eddie, come quick! You have to talk to her. She won't listen to me. I need your help!" I jumped in my car and headed toward South Central LA in response to Dolphin's call of desperation and made it to Dolphin's of Hollywood in about fifteen minutes. I bounded up the stairs to the office where I saw a most unusual sight. Petite Ruth Dolphin had her husband, "Big John," the size of an NFL lineman, backed into a corner. She was yelling all manner of accusations in language that would curl hair.

"Eddie, do something," he pleaded. "She won't let me go downstairs."

"Ruth, it will be all right. Calm down," I said in my most soothing tone, trying to hide my utter surprise and the inward smile that was forcing its way to the corners of my mouth because of the scene. I knew Ruth had high regard for me, which worked in my favor in getting her to back away from John. She eventually agreed to leave with me, and I drove her to my home. I wasn't concerned about the issue because I was already well aware of her husband's reputation for womanizing and shady business deals.

Once at my house, we continued to talk for about twenty minutes, and I eventually saw the fury leave her eyes, but the hurt remained.

In another incident, he called me to his home. When I pulled up, John and Ruth were outside and he was barely dressed. Ruth had thrown all his expensive suits on the lawn and was calmly hosing them down as if watering a garden. Incidents like this were rare and certainly not typical of Ruth's sweet personality. It's just that Dolphin's slippery side sometimes sent people over the edge, including lovely Ruth.

Despite his flaws, Dolphin became a valued friend and colleague. I partnered with him on a few of his artist concert ventures and at times witnessed the opposite side of his "fearless brute" persona. I remember we had to make a quick trip to San Diego, and I told John we didn't have time to drive and suggested we fly. He had never flown, and it took me hours to convince him to fly. Once on the plane, he was like a little kid he was so frightened. When we landed, he got down on his knees, even in his best suit, and kissed the ground, embarrassing me and everyone else around him.

John Dolphin's murder on February 1, 1958, was a shock to me, although it seemed to have been anticipated by many in the music business, an "only a matter of time" feeling. I first heard it on the radio and later read that he was shot behind his desk at his recording company office on Pico Boulevard by "frustrated singer Percy Ivy." Apparently Ivy had submitted several songs to Dolphin and after about a month had not received the promised payment. He confronted Dolphin, an argument ensued, and Dolphin was shot several times.

After his death, Ruth, who was also his business partner as well as wife, took over the company—the record stores and recording business—and I understand she made Dolphin's ventures even more successful.

After leaving Central Record Sales, I became completely involved in the national record business and moved outside the Los Angeles city area. Unfortunately I lost personal contact with John and Ruth Dolphin, but I understand that Ruth eventually sold all of her interests in Dolphin Music Enterprises sometime during the 1970s. In 2008, I read in the *Los Angeles Times* that Ruth Dolphin had died at the age of eighty-one.

John and Ruth Dolphin were business associates and personal friends who created memories for me that will always stay in the forefront of my mind. I even used John's innovative radio/record promotion and sales approach in one of my important business ventures, which turned out to be quite successful.

CHAPTER FIVE

HEART STRINGS

Why the song became a national hit baffles many people to this day. The words aren't profound in any way, and the tune, somewhat of a ditty, was unlike anything that had come out in the mid '50s. But experience taught me that most music buyers were always searching for something different, so I wasn't surprised when the country loved my song.

I co-wrote "Hearts of Stone," I'll admit, out of a secret desire to be a songwriter. It was the one song that solidified my career on the artistic side of the music business, the song that opened tons of radio station doors for me, and the song for which I've received recognition awards from numerous music organizations, including the prestigious Broadcast Music, Inc.

The year was 1954. I was still at Central Record Sales Company making one of my regular calls on Dolphin's of Hollywood. An acquaintance, Johnny Torrance, from San Bernardino, would often hang around the store trying to introduce new songs by a gospel-turned-doo-wop group he managed.

"We really need a record store like this one in San Bernardino," he'd always say. "We don't have anything like this there."

I thought he might be onto something, and since I was always on the lookout for new opportunities, I listened. Torrance and I eventually became good friends and then business partners. I took him up on his idea of a record store in San Bernardino, and we soon opened Paradise Records in the downtown area.

However, to be like Dolphin's of Hollywood, we needed a radio show in the window, so we held auditions for a DJ. One of those auditioning was a young man named Rudy Jackson, who happened to be the lead singer in Torrance's group. He did all right, but we decided to go with someone else for the DJ role, someone with more experience that was already on the radio.

Torrance and I agreed that his doo-wop group, with Jackson as the lead, had potential, and so we named them the Jewels. There were five members, and they had a sound similar to all the hit groups coming out of the East Coast. Through my association with Torrance and the Jewels, Rudy Jackson and I started casually putting together songs, a way to fulfill my desire for songwriting. He'd come up with the melody, and I'd put words to it, or vice versa. One day we came up with "Hearts of Stone."

I felt so strongly about this song that I decided to produce it myself, which I had learned how to do during my early career days at Aladdin Records. I also created a new record label with two acquaintances who had a record publishing company, Larry Goldberg and Al Schlesinger. We named the label R & B Records. I pretty much knew the ropes and was also fortunate to know a genius of a musician named Ernie Freeman, who I asked to do the arrangement for "Hearts of Stone."

"I can't do this. This is not right," Freeman complained when trying to write out the parts for the song. He was talking about the beats and measures that weren't making sense to him.

"You've got too many bars here. Then the melody—"

I cut him off. "Ernie, musically you're right, but I want to go for the overall feel. I just want to go for the feel." Freeman ended up doing a fantastic job with the song, albeit, reluctantly.

I had the perfect setup for distribution and promotion of "Hearts of Stone" in the Los Angeles area. I was already with Central Records, the number one record distributor in Southern California, so I worked out a good deal with Jim Warren, owner of Central. I could also promote and sell the record through our own record store and radio show in San Bernardino. So right out of the blocks we sold more than fifty thousand records. But that was just regionally, in the Southern California area. Even though I was very familiar with the major independent record distributing companies in the US, my label, R & B Records, was undercapitalized to adequately distribute the record nationally.

One day Harry Goodman stopped by Central Records, which he did occasionally because he was friends with Warren. Harry was the base player in the orchestra of his famous brother, Benny Goodman. Benny and Harry had another brother named Gene, who owned a major music publishing company in New York. He published a lot of hit songs, especially the East Coast doo-wop and R & B songs. Harry hooked me up with Gene.

"Look, if I can do something with 'Hearts of Stone,' I'd like to make a deal with you," Gene offered.

Since the song wasn't doing anything nationally anyway, my partner and I figured we didn't have anything to lose, so we agreed. Several weeks later, Goodman called.

"Eddie, I can get the song recorded by a group out of Tennessee called the Fontaine Sisters." He also could get a country artist to do it named Red Foley, who was Pat Boone's father-in-law. He didn't stop there. Goodman could also get an R & B group from Cincinnati to record it named The Charms.

My partners and I agreed to a copublishing deal with Goodman's music publishing company, Regent Music, and the result was "Hearts of Stone" becoming a tremendous national hit song. It became a number one pop hit record by the Fontaine Sisters; number one on the TV show *Your Hit Parade* for seven consecutive weeks; a number one record in the country field by Red Foley; and number one in R & B by The Charms. It was number one in each genre of music simultaneously—the first song to ever do this.

"Hearts of Stone" has been recorded by thirty-two different artists over the years. It became a national hit for the second time seven years later as an instrumental record by the Bill Black Combo out of Memphis. Then several years later, for the third time it entered the national record charts again by John Fogerty.

"Hearts of Stone" is on the soundtracks of several movies, including the hit movie *Good Fellas*. The song is almost sixty years old and still generating a considerable amount of royalties.

Perhaps "Hearts of Stone" was a hit because unlike most contemporary songs of that era, the lyrics of "Hearts of Stone" allude to someone rejecting love rather than searching for love or lamenting over a lost love. As co-writers, Rudy Jackson and I dared to be different, both lyrically and musically.

My career took me away from home quite a bit, maybe more than what was prudent for a man with a family in the 1950s. My wife Tessie and I had our first son, Eddie Jr., in 1948. His brother Donald came four years later. Both were healthy, happy boys. Then our beautiful daughter, Teresa Lynn, was born and immediately stole her father's heart, as baby girls often do. But something was wrong. As Teresa Lynn grew, instead of speaking, she just made noises, like baby sounds. Physically she was fine, but she couldn't talk. We took her to every psychiatrist and psychologist available to us, but to no avail. The one catch-all term used back then was mental retardation. Today it may be diagnosed as a form of autism—I don't know. She was never able to speak clearly, except to say in her way, *Daddy, Eddie, Donnie, Tessie,* and other words that only family members could understand.

We all did our best to give Teresa Lynn a normal life. All of her doctors and eventually I suggested to Tessie that our daughter be placed in an institution, which understandably did not sit well with Tessie.

"She will get better. Why can't we take care of her at home?" Tessie pleaded.

"She needs more than what we can provide," I said. "She may make more progress in a place with a trained staff, with other children like her. Besides, you can't handle all this by yourself, because I have to travel a lot."

I was of the opinion that once we did everything we could do, it was time to make decisions that would be more beneficial to Teresa in the long term and not for our own personal desires. Being a loving, caring mother, it was too difficult for Tessie to agree.

There was always a delicate balance between my career and my family. Tessie never enthusiastically embraced my career dreams and aspirations as I did and seldom showed a real interest in my work. She directed most of her interests and energies toward our children and our home.

We had a big, beautiful home and our children went to the best schools, but if it meant that I had to be in New York on Thanksgiving Day, I was in New York on Thanksgiving Day. And since Tessie rarely wanted to travel with me or go to any of the record industry affairs, we too often lived separate lives.

As my career progressed on a steep incline, my marriage was on an opposite decline, and after almost eighteen years, Tessie and I went our separate ways. It was an amicable divorce, and afterward we both continued to give our love and devotion to the health and well-being of our children, and especially to Teresa. I also remained very close to Tessie's family, who had become like my real family through the years. Many years after the divorce, Tessie passed away.

Teresa grew up to become a beautiful young woman, but forever remained mentally and emotionally a child. Several years after her mother's death, Teresa also passed away. In memory of my loving daughter I wrote this prose:

OFTEN ON MY MIND...FOREVER IN MY HEART

My sweet, little angel daughter
was sent into our lives with imperfections of body and mind
but with a special heart and soul that could only
have been heavenly divined.

She was born with vocal chords forever muted
But spoke eloquently with her smiling eyes,
with her tight hugs and soft kisses,
and with her warm, loving heart.

She loved to wear beautiful, colorful clothes,
often changing several times a day,
while listening to her favorite music
and joyfully dancing any sadness in her life away.

Suddenly one day, much too soon in her short life,
like a beautiful, peaceful dove, she flew away
to be with her mother and Holy Father
in their heavenly home above.

My heart is sad and lonely without her,
but I am also happy for my little darling
because I know that she is happily listening to the music of
the angels
and joyfully dancing with her mother, forevermore!

Some hearts may be made of stone, but definitely not mine.

CHAPTER SIX

BEHIND THE IMPERIAL THRONE

The press said I wouldn't last sixty days at Imperial Records. They were off by about nine years. The problem, as they saw it, was owner Lew Chudd. The press had witnessed numerous careers cut off at the knees by Lew, whom they described as shrewd, ruthless, yet astute. I obviously didn't have a problem with him, but I certainly understood why those words were a fitting description.

Imperial Records was a major independent record company in California, known for having three of the hottest stars of the 1950s—Fats Domino, Ricky Nelson, and Slim Whitman. The company also produced hits by Ernie Freeman, Irma Thomas, Billy J. Kramer, Smiley Lewis, Johnny Rivers, Sandy Nelson, and dozens of others.

I was riding pretty high in my career in the mid-1950s, with "Hearts of Stone" being the number one hit in pop music, country, and R & B. Plus I was instrumental in Central Records becoming one of the top three record distributors in the nation. It wasn't even ranked when I first came to the company. So Imperial was one of several national record companies recruiting me, along with companies in Chicago, Detroit, and New York. I came pretty close to being able to write my own ticket, but I chose Imperial for one main reason—because the headquarters was in Hollywood and I didn't want to leave sunny California.

In February 1955 I resigned from Central Record Sales and joined Imperial Records, despite what I heard about Lew Chudd. Actually, I first met Chudd when I was still at Central Records, and I didn't particularly like him. He was a little guy who looked to me like a miniature Abraham Lincoln, with deep-set eyes and high cheek bones. All he needed was a stovepipe hat and maybe five or six more inches. Chudd's father, a Russian-Jewish immigrant, was even named Abraham.

Chudd had started Imperial Records in the mid-1940s and focused on authentic Mexican and folk music. He had "branched out" into square dancing records, wedding albums, gypsy music, and Dixieland jazz.

One day at Central Records, he came in to meet with me and owner Jim Warren to talk about distribution. He turned to me and said, "Well, my records aren't the type of records that would sell on Central Avenue," which I took as another snide remark about the black community in LA.

I said, "Well, from what I can see, your records aren't the type of records that would sell no damn place. That's why you're not selling any."

But despite our less than cordial first encounter, I eventually went to work for Chudd at Imperial, becoming his new national director of promotion and sales, a fancy title that simply meant I did just about everything. Author Rick Coleman in his book *Blue Monday* recounted my hiring at Imperial:

> At Imperial, the big news in February was Chudd's hiring of Eddie Ray, a black salesman at L.A.'s Central Record Sales, to head promotions. *Cash Box* called the hiring the "biggest news to hit the music field in several months." African Americans in management positions at white companies were almost nonexistent. Now, along with Dave Bartholomew, Chudd had *two* in his tiny record company...*Cash Box* wished Ray "good luck in his new venture," likely implying the nearly impossible task of getting along with the caustic Chudd. Though record men bet that he would last at Imperial at most sixty days, the soft-spoken Ray developed a working relationship with Chudd that lasted as long as the company.

Ironically, Imperial turned out to be my longest tenure at any company. And what Imperial did for me was launch my career as a record executive on the national scene. I was involved in all phases of the business—sales, promotion, distribution, A & R, publishing, manufacturing—every aspect.

Lew Chudd wasn't what you'd call a record man, someone into music, the artists, or the creative side of things. He was a businessman. He would come into the office early every morning, and it took me months to figure out why. It finally dawned on me—the New York Stock Market. He'd come in early to buy and sell stock. Records to him, in his words, were like toilet stools.

"If you manufacture them, you sell them," he'd quip. "You sell whatever you have." His all-business approach wasn't just to get a jump on the stock market or to make profitable deals for the company. It was ingrained in his abrupt personality.

Imperial Records was located inside the Warner Theater Building, in the heart of Hollywood at Hollywood Boulevard and Wilcox, above the original famous Hollywood Walk of Fame. It was also a couple of blocks from the Roosevelt Hotel where the popular TV show *This Is Your Life* was running as well as not far from the famous Grauman's Chinese Theater. In the 1950s the boulevard was a very clean street filled with tourists who thought they'd see stars walking up and down the street—of course they never would because the stars hid away in their homes in Hollywood Hills or Beverly Hills.

I'll never forget my first day on the job. I walked into the Warner Theatre Building where Imperial occupied part of the fourth floor. My sizeable office had big picture windows overlooking the boulevard. I remember at holiday time my kids and their friends would come to my office to watch the big Hollywood Christmas Parade. That's the rare time the tourists would see the stars on the boulevard, in the parade.

So I walked into Imperial and as with any first day on the job, you'd expect some kind of orientation, or at least a little background on where things stood with your area of responsibility. I began to ask the few staff members about distributorships and radio stations, but I got nowhere. No one knew anything. Finally I walked into Lew Chudd's office.

"Lew, who do I talk to about your radio lists, DJ lists, and so forth?"

Barely looking in my direction, he coldly responded, "That's what you're here for. You establish it."

Here I was, in a big Hollywood office, the media taking bets on my longevity, and all I got from Abe Lincoln was, "You establish it."

The second day, still nobody said anything about what happens at the office. *I see right now I'm going to have to just do.* I approached Chudd again. "Look, Lew, I want to go on a trip. I want to meet the distributors."

"Fine," he said. "Talk to Edna. She'll book your flight. She'll do anything for you," and he walked away.

Then before I got on the road, I tried a third time. "Lew, your distributor list? Does your distributor for that area have a DJ list, a radio station list? Do they have built-in promotions people?"

He turned to me and with a hint of exasperation said, "Eddie, you'll find that out when you get there." That was it.

As I worked my way across the country, I found out that not much was in place for Imperial as far as distribution was concerned, except in big cities like Chicago and New York City. But the one thing I did find out before going on the road was that Chudd was angry with the distributor in Baltimore for some reason. In fact he wanted me to switch to a larger distributor in nearby Washington, Swartz Brothers, which I was familiar with from my days at Aladdin Records.

Upon arriving in Baltimore, I paid a visit to see our distributor, Mangold Distributing Company. I spent time with the owner, Manny Goldberg, and promotion man Eddie Kalicka and, to my surprise, got an earful from them.

"Nobody from Imperial has spoken with us in six months. Records come in the back door of new artists, and we don't know who the hell the new artists are. We don't receive any paperwork on them," Kalicka complained. He went on. "The only correspondence we get from Imperial are these nasty letters from some guy named JJ, screaming about getting his checks. Who is this JJ?" I was clueless. I didn't know anybody at Imperial with the initials JJ. I came to find out later that

JJ was the fictitious name Lew Chudd used when he wrote scathing letters.

Part of the problem with distributors was our payment policy called "2/10 EOM," meaning distributors would get a 2 percent discount if they paid us within ten days after the end of the month. Well, Chudd considered ten days late, but distributors didn't, and neither did I for that matter. So Lew would send out these late letters under his fictitious name. Kalicka continued his rant, calling JJ every name in the book.

I called Chudd. "Look, Lew, I'm very impressed with the promotion man and the owner here in Baltimore." I didn't tell him about all the terrible things they were saying about him or JJ. "I think I can work with them," I said, attempting to smooth things over for both sides.

"Go back to the hotel, sleep over it," Chudd said, "and if you feel the same way in the morning, then don't change distributors." So the next morning, I still felt the same way. I didn't change distributors, and I went on to New York. I eventually arrived back at the office from my cross-country trip.

Then one day out of the clear blue, I hear "Eddie! Eddie!" It was Lew screaming my name from his office. "Didn't I tell you to change distributors in Baltimore!" he yelled. He didn't use the intercom as he normally would.

I'd been at Imperial a little less than two months at this point and thought, *OK, this isn't going to work. First of all, nobody talks to me that way.* I made my way to his office and calmly said, "Wait a minute, Lew. You and I had a discussion about this. You know what I think, Lew? Perhaps we both made a mistake. Why don't we call it quits now?"

"Now you're being a kid," he responded. "Sit down." And that was the last time he ever screamed at me. He never questioned me after that time because I made it clear that there was no way I was going to stay there with that kind of treatment. I guess the press's prediction of a brief sixty-day tenure was almost true with that incident.

I soon went back on the road visiting our distributors as well as disc jockeys in some of the major cities. When in Philadelphia I'd stop by radio station WFIL and talk with a young DJ whose popularity was on a fast track since he sometimes substituted as host of an afternoon teen dance show at the station's sister television outlet. That show was called *Bob Horn's Bandstand*, and the young DJ was Richard Wagstaff Clark, better known as Dick Clark. He became full-time host of the show in 1956, and it was soon picked up by ABC as *American Bandstand* and went national in 1957.

But just three years later, Clark's reputation was tainted a bit when he was called to testify in the so-called Payola hearings.

During the 1950's, because disc jockeys wielded so much decision-making power over what records were played, a number of them began to cash in on their influence by accepting "pay-for-play" or what was dubbed *payola*. As a 2005 article in *Performing Songwriter* described it, "Aware of their rising status, jocks established flat rate deals with labels and record distributors. A typical deal for a mid-level DJ was $50 a week, per record, to ensure a minimum amount of spins. More influential jocks commanded percentages of grosses for local concerts, lavish trips, free records by the boxful (some even opened their own record stores), plus all the time-honored swag…In November 1959, in closed and open sessions before the U.S. House Oversight Committee, 335 disc jockeys from around the country admitted to having received over $263,000 in 'consulting fees.'

That figure was only the tip of the payola iceberg (before the hearings, Phil Lind, a DJ at Chicago's WAIT had confessed that he had once taken $22,000 to play a single record. The trial heated up when the two most influential jocks in the country took the stand."

Those two disc jockeys were Dick Clark and Alan Freed (Freed worked at WABC radio). While both denied engaging in the shady payola practice, when it was all said and done, Clark received a pass and Freed was charged with commercial bribery, fined, and fired from WABC radio, but he escaped jail time. Some asserted that the personalities of the two DJs made all the difference with the congressional committee. Freed was seen as abrasive and uncooperative, while Clark was called "a fine young man" by committee chairman Oren Harris.

Through the years people asked me about payola and some boldly asked if I was involved in it. My answer was always an unequivocal "absolutely not," although I was aware of it, as was anyone in the record business during that time. What people don't realize is that in 1950 there were only about 250 disc jockeys in the country, but by 1957, when I was at Imperial, the number had grown to over 5,000, so not all of them were on the take. And when I had DJs like John Dolphin calling me to purchase records by the thousand, payola, at least where I was concerned, was a nonissue.

Clark survived the scandal, and whether it was his "famously ingratiating demeanor," as some described it, that made the difference, or the fact that just prior to the hearings he divested himself of his record company holdings, or both, I can't say. What we do know is that Clark went on to fame and fortune afterward.

Many years after I first encountered Clark when he was a young DJ in Philadelphia, I saw him again at a Las Vegas restaurant, and to my surprise he came to my table, excited to see me. After greeting me warmly, he went back to his table and brought his guests over to meet me, as though I were the celebrity. I experienced then as before that "famously ingratiating demeanor." Clark's popularity through the decades was evidenced by the outpouring of sympathy at his death on April 18, 2012. It immediately took me back to those days at Imperial when I met him.

So it wasn't payola that was an issue for me when on the road, but it was some of Lew Chudd's idiosyncrasies. For instance he asked me to start sending him written reports of where I'd been or what stations I'd visited. I would, like an idiot, go to the public stenographers they had at hotels in those days and send back a glowing detailed report. I soon found out that Chudd didn't even read the reports. He'd simply tell the secretary to file it. One day I asked him about it.

"Look, Lew, why do I go through the trouble of sending you all this information and you don't even read it?"

"First of all, you should do it so you'll be familiar with what you've done," he replied. "Second, I don't have to read it to know what you've done. I'll know when this month's statement comes in."

After that, I really didn't discuss much with him. I'd just do what I wanted. I didn't send any more reports, and he basically stayed out of my way, except for our occasional chats at Coffee Dan's or some other nearby eatery.

During one of these chats, I shared with him some of the positive press I was getting, especially in light of the initial dire predictions. His response was, "Well that along with fifteen cents will buy you a cup of coffee." Lew Chudd wasn't a hand holder nor ego stroker, and since I didn't need either, we got along fine. I think he didn't like the positive press, because he thought I'd get better offers, which I already had been, but I chose to stay at Imperial. Again, Hollywood. Sunny California.

Chudd was the type of boss who wouldn't tell his people they were doing a good job, at least not to their face, but would speak highly of them to others. So word would get back to me. But it really wasn't so much what he said but his actions that told me how well he thought of me. In fact, one of the things I really appreciated about Chudd was how he'd back up his people.

I'll never forget the time I was in Buffalo, New York, when I was promoting one of our popular artists. There was a big disc jockey up there, but our distributor had close ties with another disc jockey. When a particular hit record came out, I gave the big disc jockey a two-day exclusive on the new record. He was playing it like crazy, and our distributor was getting all kinds of calls for orders.

However, the disc jockey with ties to our distributor called him and read him the riot act. The distributor, probably at a loss for what to do, decided to blame me. He called Chudd, ranting, "Eddie Ray has fouled things up! Oh, he's messed things up real good. He doesn't know what he's doing. I'm dead in this market…" and so forth and so on.

When the man finished, Chudd simply responded, "Pack up all of our records and ship them back to me. You're no longer my distributor." That's the way Chudd was. That's what I liked about the guy. Also at times he was quite amusing. For instance, during our chats I'd sometimes share with him what was going on in this or that market, some interesting news about a particular distributor. A few weeks later, he'd call me and say, "Eddie, meet me down at Coffee Dan's," and he'd proceed to tell me the same news I'd told him. He didn't realize I was the one who told him.

Sometimes what he had to share at our informal meetings brought an internal rush of pride for me—pride from quickly helping Imperial reach some defining milestones. For instance, once when I had been at the company for only about a year, I was in New York and didn't know Chudd was also in town. He was at another hotel.

"Eddie, let's go have breakfast." He told me to meet him at some swanky hotel. He insisted that we always stay at first-class hotels and fly first class. I never traveled coach while at Imperial, and that was highly unusual for someone working for an independent record company.

At breakfast he excitedly said, "Eddie, this is our first ten-million-dollar month!" When I joined him, he never had even a one-million-dollar month.

I smiled because I knew that I was instrumental in taking a small label that sold primarily Mexican, folk, and square dancing music to a nationally recognized label. I also knew the timing was perfect for me to join Imperial because of the new artists I had the privilege of promoting—two of them being Fats Domino and Ricky Nelson.

Eddie Ray and the Central Records Sales staff. (Los Angeles, CA, early 1950s)

Eddie Ray with his two sons, Eddie Ray, Jr. and Donald L. Ray. (Los Angeles, CA, 1958)

My first wife, Tessie Johnson Ray.

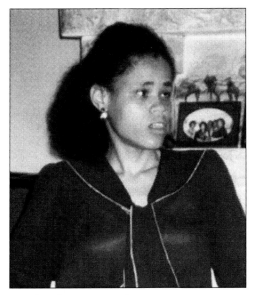

My daughter, Teresa Ray.

Jim Warren (Central Record Sales), Eddie Ray (Central Record Sales and later head of Imperial Records' promotions), Lew Chudd, Fats Domino, Dave Bartholomew, Cliff Aaronson.

Eddie Ray and Irma Thomas reunited after working together at Imperial Records, at the Rock and Roll Hall of Fame. (Cleveland, OH, November 12, 2010)

National Songwriters Hall of Fame songwriter and Grammy Award-winning record producer Allen Toussaint and Eddie Ray reunited at a tribute ceremony for Dave Bartholomew in New Orleans.

Eddie Ray and Imperial Records internationally award winning drummer Sandy Nelson. (1959)

Capitol-Tower Records executives, Gordon Bud Fraser, President; Eddie Ray, VP A & R; Perry Mayer, VP Publicity and PR. (Hollywood, CA, 1965)

With Bob Summers, record producer, and Mike Curb, record producer, signing movie soundtrack agreement with Capitol-Tower Records. (mid-1960s)

Eddie Ray, VP of Capitol Records. (1966)

Eddie Ray, MGM Records, and award-winning jazz organist Jimmy Smith. (Los Angeles, CA, early 1970s)

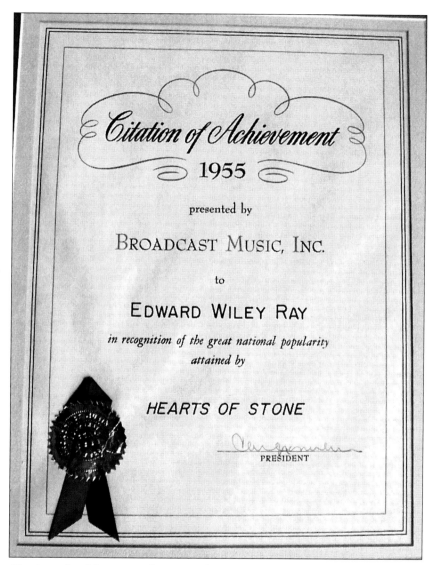

Citation of Achievement from BMI for "Hearts of Stone."

Hall of Fame producer Dave Bartholomew, President of BMI Frances
Preston and Eddie Ray.

CHAPTER SEVEN

To Know Fats Domino

T alking with Fats Domino was like pulling teeth sometimes. He was extremely shy, reclusive in fact, which
surprised a lot of DJs and reporters who attempted
to interview him through the years. His stage persona that
could work a club into a frenzy and his true personality were
miles apart.

Lew Chudd signed Domino to the Imperial label in 1949
as I was about to join Central Record Sales the following year.
By 1953, while still at Central, I was part of a group photo of
Chudd, presenting Domino with two gold records representing
two million records sold. The photo of me, Domino, Chudd,
Central's owner Jim Warren, and several others ended up on
the cover of *Cash Box* magazine. But two million records was
just the tip of the iceberg for the rising star, whom I wouldn't
officially meet until I joined Imperial a couple years later.

Fats Domino, whose real first name was Antoine, was synonymous with New Orleans. He loved the city, loved the people, loved the music, and they loved him. But like with many musicians, he wasn't an overnight success. People fail to realize the arduous path musicians endure before they reach stardom. Domino struggled as a young artist to gain a foothold in the vibrant New Orleans music scene in the mid-1940s. He paid his dues in hole-in-the-wall black clubs around town.

As I look back at my career, I can say I'm proud of the fact that I was instrumental in Domino being one of the megastars of all time. When I arrived at Imperial, I immediately started a national promotion for him, which penetrated the crossover, or white, market. I would take his records to any and all radio stations, not just to R & B stations. I guess that's why people considered me a maverick. But to me it didn't take a rocket scientist to figure out that the power of record sales, at that time, rested with the radio stations. Get the record played. That's where I concentrated. The relationships I built through the years with radio DJs across the country resulted in the records I handled being played.

For instance, when I was still at Central, I had a great relationship with Hunter Hancock, a popular white DJ in Los Angeles. Central's owner Jim Warren would buy time on Hancock's station, KGFJ. Hancock would be the DJ during those slots, and I'd write his scripts each week telling him what to play. I even had him put on some new artists that Central didn't carry, which only heightened the popularity of his show. It was those kinds of relationships that I was able to leverage once at Imperial.

Once whites heard Domino on their stations, they started requesting his songs from the DJs, jukeboxes, and record stores. The snowball effect took over, and Domino's sales skyrocketed. The two million that he was congratulated for in the 1953 photo ballooned to 110 million records sold throughout his career.

However, while Domino loved performing, he loathed being on the road. Maybe it was his shyness, or the effects of segregation when his band in the early days couldn't eat in restaurants, or his lack of a high school education that made him uncomfortable. Whatever the reason, when we'd travel together, he wouldn't venture far from the hotel, preferring to cook one of his favorite Creole dishes in his room—red beans and rice. And when I was to meet Domino for an engagement, I wasn't sure what he'd do, whether he'd even show up, because sometimes he didn't. That's just the way he was.

When Katrina hit New Orleans in 2005, the news reported how Domino rode out the storm in his Lower Ninth Ward home and had to be rescued by boat. At first he was feared missing until his daughter saw a newspaper photo of his rescue. I wasn't surprised by a quote of him saying, "I don't think I'll ever leave the Ninth Ward."

It took me back to a very brief conversation I had with Domino in the back of a limo on our way to an engagement— one of those "pulling teeth" talks.

"Hey, Fats, why don't you get a beautiful home in Beverly Hills? You could live on one of the highest hills there," I encouraged. Back then a home in Beverly Hills would cost several hundred thousand dollars and be worth three or four million today.

After a moment, Domino replied, "Look, Eddie, I appreciate everything that you guys are doing for me at the record company. I appreciate what you tell me about recording, about promotion and the sales of my records, but when it comes to my personal living…" His voice dropped off. After he said that, I never brought it up again.

Domino wanted to live in the neighborhood where he was born, went to school, and started his musical career. He built a million-dollar split-level mansion, referred to as the "big house," right there, displacing several of the modest shotgun houses. What's interesting, though, is that even with the mansion where his wife and family stayed, he preferred to live next door, in one of the shotgun houses. As he told *Blue Monday* author Rick Coleman, he loved his wife and family but needed a little breathing space. My heart really went out to him when I read Coleman's account of Katrina's devastation:

> I entered Domino's famed house where I had visited with him on several honored occasions. Though it had been flooded to the ceiling, from the outside both it and the "big house" next door looked relatively undamaged. As I walked through the dark gutted building in eerie silence, phantoms called out to me—the musical legacies of Domino, the Ninth Ward, New Orleans. There in the gloom at the back of the house barely lighted by reflected sunlight was the only piece of furniture—the remains of Domino's couch built from the back of a Cadillac, the car that symbolized musical stardom in the 1950s.

I then thought about happier times with Domino and how his spur-of-the-moment musical whims could result in a hit record. I'll never forget the day I was in a hotel room in Philadelphia with Domino and his producer, Dave Bartholomew. Fats had gotten a letter from the IRS, and we were kidding him. Then either he or Dave said, "Well, you know what that means. Instead of flying back to New Orleans, this time you're going to be walking back home." Then in the room, right there was the creation of the song, "I'm Walkin'," which became one of his biggest hits.

While the talent of greats like Fats Domino held my admiration, I was equally fascinated by the musical gifts of those behind the stars, like his producer Bartholomew. People in the music industry will recognize Bartholomew's name because he's been inducted into just about every musical hall of fame there is, and many people, especially from New Orleans, will have been fortunate enough to experience his musical genius. I was.

CHAPTER EIGHT

Dynamic Duo

The *New Orleans Sound.* Just mention it and people know what you're talking about. Whether their mind's ear hears sultry blues, soulful R & B, or smooth jazz, the rhythm of the brass is unmistakable. For people in the south, especially in New Orleans, that distinctive horn comes from the lips of trumpeter extraordinaire Dave Bartholomew. He's credited with being the architect, the father of the *New Orleans Sound.*

I'd have to say that in the 1950s Bartholomew was one of the top three trumpet players in the nation, actually among the top five in the world. What many people don't know is he was also a top producer, arranger, and songwriter whose musical genius was instrumental in Fats Domino hits such as "Ain't That a Shame," "Blueberry Hill," "I'm Walkin'," and many others.

He produced for Domino and other artists while in the employ of Lew Chudd, owner of Imperial Records, which is where I met him. Chudd first heard the trumpeter in 1947 in Houston on one of his talent scouting trips. Bartholomew was in the city with his popular band finishing up a multiweek engagement at a night club before returning home to New Orleans. After the show, Chudd approached Bartholomew with his intention to hire him as an artist and producer for Imperial. He finally brought him on board a couple years later, along with Domino, whom the trumpeter had introduced to Chudd.

The Domino-Bartholomew "dynamic duo" came out with hit after hit. The two co-wrote songs not only for Domino but other artists, like Smiley Lewis's "I Hear You Knockin'," and songs recorded by pop artists such as Elvis Presley. While at Imperial, the trumpeter-producer had a career high of million sellers, close to twenty, with nine of them consecutive. In later years he was inducted into just about every hall of fame imaginable—the Rock and Roll, Rhythm and Blues, Louisiana Music, the Songwriters—all of these hall of fames as well as being Songwriter of the Year for Broadcast Music, Inc. (BMI), a performance rights organization. He achieved more awards than one can count. I was his guest at each of his hall of fame inductions, and he introduced me as mostly responsible for his music industry success, which was a special honor coming from Bartholomew who seldom spoke positively about anybody!

So much musical talent in one man obviously didn't happen overnight. As Bartholomew tells it, "I would hang around my father's barber shop as a kid, and one day a man named Peter Davis, who used to teach kids to play instruments, gave me a secondhand trumpet. I worried that man to death to teach me everything because I wanted to be like Louis Armstrong. That's all I wanted, to be like Louis Armstrong," he recalls.

Davis, who had actually taught Armstrong, took little Dave under his wing, and by the time he was twelve, Bartholomew was sitting in with his father's bands, then working the riverboats as a young teen. But it was in the army where his musical craft was really honed.

"I was in the army for three-and-a-half years and worked with some great musicians, nothing but professionals," Bartholomew says. "I learned to write music, arrange, and compose." With military bands he toured all over Europe. After his stint in the army, Dave went back to New Orleans and put together his band, *Dave Bartholomew and His Orchestra.* "For many months, I had the best band in New Orleans." It was that band Chudd heard that led to Bartholomew being with Imperial for almost twenty years.

Dave Bartholomew and I became very good friends, lifelong family friends. While at Imperial he, like Domino, worked from New Orleans, refusing to move to California. One day I got him to agree to come on a promotional trip with me. These trips consisted of a packed schedule beginning before sunrise and ending late at night watching a performance at a club.

On this particular trip with Bartholomew, we began in San Francisco, then went to Denver, on to Chicago, then down to Atlanta, Miami, and back over to Dallas. At each stop we'd have a breakfast meeting with a distributor or some other industry contact, sales meetings over lunch, meetings with managers and artists in the afternoon, then later visit the night DJs and end at a club. We'd start all over the next day.

Bartholomew hated the schedule. Like most artists he was accustomed to working at night and sleeping during the day, so by the time we reached Dallas, he said, "Eddie, I don't see how in the world you do this. I'm going home!" He also hated a habit I had that I didn't give up until years later—cigar smoking. Bartholomew never smoked anything, which made sense given his powerful trumpeter lungs. At the end of this whirlwind trip, he said emphatically, "Eddie Ray, the reason I'll never go with you anymore is because I don't like the schedule you guys keep, but more importantly, I can't stand those damn cigars you smoke!"

Today when reminiscing about our travels, Bartholomew is more complimentary, giving me credit for much of his success. "Eddie Ray could sell anything. He had gotten our records played where no one else could," he comments. "Everybody loved Eddie. We'd go to One Stops and people would say, 'What does Eddie think?' 'What does Eddie say?' 'Has Eddie heard this?' 'Does he like it?' Eddie was *the man*. Everybody knew he could pick the tunes. He had a commercial mind."

Of course Bartholomew gave me a lot to work with during those years. He was a perfectionist in the studio and didn't expect anything less from his musicians. He was very tough on them, and everything had to be done exactly the way Dave wanted it done. The horn player had to play it this way. The drummer had to do it this way, and if they didn't, he would penalize the musician by not hiring him for awhile. He'd put him on hiatus for about six or seven sessions, replacing him with someone else during that time, but that's what it took to come out with million sellers.

Bartholomew was also tough on the artists, and a lot of them would write letters to Lew Chudd complaining Dave this and Dave that. Chudd would come to me and hand me the letter. After I read it, he'd say, "Eddie, what kind of options do we have on this artist's contract?" or "When is the contract due to be released? Have we already fulfilled the requirements?

What happens if we release the artist before the end of the contract?" I'd provide all the information, and then we'd send the artist a letter informing them that they were being released from Imperial Records. We all knew Bartholomew was one of a kind, and Chudd would let artists go before he'd touch Dave.

Dave and I did take more trips together, and some turned out to be quite interesting. I'll never forget when we went to a small black club in Atlanta. As with most clubs, everybody at their tables was talking and drinking, but there was a comedian up front, doing his act. Nobody was paying attention to the guy. I kind of felt sorry for him because he was being ignored by the audience. But we started listening and realized he was really funny. He told long stories, not quick one-liners. So after his performance I mentioned to Dave that we should record the guy. I went up and introduced myself to the comedian and told him what I had in mind. He told me where he was staying, which turned out to be a fleabag hole-in-the-wall hotel down the street. The next day I went there. He was all by himself, in this dank little room. I explained about Imperial and the artists we had and discussed doing a comedy album with him. In those days I carried a standard contract and went over it with him. He was very interested, so I signed him.

Two weeks later, we flew the comedian to New Orleans to work with Bartholomew. He spent a few weeks with Dave and recorded the album. Imperial released the album, but it really didn't do anything for us and we didn't do much with it, so it basically remained on the shelf.

Then just a few years later, the comedian became a smash hit, with his own national TV show that he retained the rights to, making him a multimillionaire. He was none other than Flip Wilson. Wilson was one of America's most popular entertainers in the late '60s and early '70s and the first

African-American performer to catch on as host of a major weekly network variety show with *The Flip Wilson Show*. Just about anyone who watched TV during those years will remember the characters he created, most famously "Geraldine" with her favorite quips, "The devil made me do it" and "What you see is what you get."

Bartholomew and I today still laugh, shaking our heads in disbelief about our Flip Wilson story.

The timing of signing artists was sometimes hit or miss. While the record companies I worked for usually landed performers who came out with great hits, occasionally opportunities slipped right through my fingers. For instance, while at Imperial during a visit to our Seattle distributor, Jerry Dennon, their promotion manager, told me about a local record on a small label that was beginning to sell big in the Seattle area. I asked Jerry to arrange an appointment for me to meet the record owner so I might discuss possible acquisition. The earliest Dennon could arrange the appointment was four o'clock that day. I had a five-thirty flight to New York for an important early morning meeting the next day, but we went ahead and set the appointment for four.

However, when the record owner had not arrived for our appointment by four thirty, I told Dennon I couldn't wait any longer and had to leave for the airport. I asked him to send a copy of the record to my Hollywood office and I would follow up with the owner after listening to it.

After arriving back home and listening to the record, I immediately called the owner but was unable to reach him. I then called Dennon and said I was definitely interested in making a deal for the record, but Jerry informed me that the artist had already signed with another record company. The record became one of the biggest selling single records of all times, and is still one of the most played "golden oldies" on the radio. I had missed "Louie, Louie" by The Kingsmen.

That was the nature of the business, and it wasn't the first or last time there would be some important "misses." But when we "hit" at Imperial, we hit big, not only with talented teams like Dave Bartholomew and Fats Domino but other big names that helped build the Imperial empire.

CHAPTER NINE

NELSON AND NELSON

"How many records have I sold so far, Eddie?" The teen had stopped by my office at Imperial on his way home from Hollywood High School, a few blocks away.

"It looks great. You're up to seven hundred thousand."

"How many do I need to reach a million?" he sincerely asked.

"Well, you're at seven hundred thousand. How many do you think you need to reach a million?"

"That's why I have accountants. So I don't have to think about those things."

I just shook my head. *Poor little rich kid.*

Rick Nelson was a teenager when he signed with us at Imperial Records and was already a heartthrob. His popularity stemmed from appearing on his parents' TV show, *The*

Adventures of Ozzie and Harriett. For anyone growing up in the '50's, Ozzie and Harriett were household names and their show was a TV icon, depicting what was thought to be an ideal American family. The show lasted a record-breaking fourteen years.

To me it seemed like everything Rick's father, Ozzie Nelson, touched became golden. I have to give it to him. He was a very talented, creative guy who moved through the entertainment world at lightning speed. Ozzie started a band in college that was a hit. He met Harriett who became his vocalist and wife. The popular band ended up providing music for *The Red Skelton Show.*

Ozzie then proposed a radio show to CBS in which the Nelsons would play themselves. He directed and cowrote all the episodes, and the radio program was a big hit in the early 1940s. The Nelsons then signed a long-term contract with ABC, which premiered the TV show in 1952.

Rick, better known as Ricky as a teen, and his older brother, David, were regulars on the show, often singing at the end of each episode. During this time Rick also started to cover records of other artists, one of which was Fats Domino. Covering records was a common practice, especially when black artists would have a hit record on R & B stations. Whites would sing a version of it so it would be played on white stations. Rick did his version of Domino's "I'm Walkin'" and "Ain't that a Shame," which caught the attention of Lew Chudd. Chudd found out Rick was on a small label and offered him a better deal to sign with Imperial.

I found Rick to be a very polite young man. He was the type of youngster who, if he was sitting in my office and an adult walked in, would stand and wouldn't sit down until you'd say it was OK for him to sit. I'd never seen this with any other young artist.

Other than promoting and selling a remarkable five consecutive million-selling records by Rick, a most interesting part of my relationship with the family was with his dad. As I mentioned, everything Ozzie touched was successful—his band, TV show, kids. I understand he was even a high school coach at one time and had one of the best records of any coach in the state of New Jersey for several years. He was also a talented writer.

But Ozzie was the type of guy who took control of the studio, telling cameramen what angle to shoot, the script writers what to write, producers what to do. He would supervise every aspect of a production. At Imperial Rick's producer, Jimmy Haskell, had a lot of major hit records with the young artist, but Ozzie's overbearing presence was there second-guessing everything in the recording studio. In today's terms I guess Ozzie would be called a "control freak." He often called me at home in the evenings, rather than during office hours.

"How are Rick's records doing? How is his new record doing?" he'd inquire.

"It's going great," I'd reply. "It's been out a little over week. I've gotten sixty-five major pick hits of the week, and we're shipping four hundred to five hundred thousand a week to our distributors." I'd wait for his response.

After a moment, he'd say, "Isn't it wonderful how powerful my TV show is in selling records?" All roads led back to Ozzie Nelson. He'd never give credit to anything someone else did. Everything was his show or what he did. That's the type of guy he was.

I received a call from him on one occasion, and he was very concerned about what was happening with a new release in the New Jersey/New York area.

"I don't understand," I said. We've got it on every top station. It's selling like crazy."

"Yes, but my mother hasn't heard it for a couple of days." Evidently Ozzie's mother would monitor radio stations, especially in the New Jersey area where she lived. She called him and he in turn called me. I started to tell him what he could do with the record—he and his mother both—but naturally I didn't.

Rick's good looks and musical talent made him wildly popular, especially with young girls. He was like Elvis Presley. I remember the tons of letters we'd receive at Imperial. I couldn't believe some of the profane little girls who would send pictures of themselves naked and say all kinds of things. We got a lot of requests for photographs, which Ozzie eventually decided to handle himself through a fan club, charging for the photos. Imperial had been sending them out free.

More than occasionally Ozzie would have run-ins with some of our distributors. We had a distributor in Honolulu who was a partner with a popular radio disc jockey there. They were both involved in the promotion of one of Rick's upcoming shows. Ozzie believed the distributor was not promoting the record the way he should and didn't feel the station was playing it the way he wanted. One day he called Lew Chudd very upset.

"Lew, I don't believe it's possible for you to keep that distributor in Honolulu and keep Rick Nelson as an artist at the same time."

So Chudd called me and we went down the street to one of our favorite Hollywood Boulevard restaurants.

"You may have to go to Honolulu," Chudd said, relating the story, "to change distributors. What do you think?"

"Well, look, Lew, Rick this month represented about sixty-seven percent of our total sales. Honolulu distributors represent less than two percent of our sales, so my suggestion is I should get on a plane and go to Honolulu." But it all worked out, and we didn't have to change the distributor. A similar situation happened in Denver that worked itself out.

When it came to Ozzie and our Detroit distributor, Chudd said, "Eddie, I know what you're thinking, because we're thinking the same thing, to tell Ozzie to go jump in the lake. There's no way we're going to change our Detroit distributor!" Detroit was one of our top distributors in the country. We had had it up to our necks with Ozzie by this point, but again he was appeased in some way by a radio station and our Detroit distributor was no longer an issue.

When it came time for Rick to leave Imperial, I think everybody was ready. Because of movie deals with Warner Brothers, Ozzie decided to sign Rick with Warner's record division. He was twenty-one by this time. However, since Rick was a minor when we first signed him, under personal service contracts with minors in California, we had to pay his royalties into the courts and the court would decide how much to release to the young artist. So we had all of this money that we were holding in the courts that Ozzie didn't pay income tax on until he received it.

As he was leaving, apparently for income tax reasons, Ozzie tried to make a deal with Lew Chudd to withhold a portion of the royalty payments to subsequent accounting periods. But instead, Chudd gave it all to him in one day, in one check. Ozzie was extremely upset with Lew, and that's how their relationship ended.

Unfortunately Ozzie's golden touch didn't extend far enough to keep Rick's record career from descending for several years after he left Imperial, or keep him from reportedly being consumed by drugs for a time. He eventually came out with his first major hit record in over a decade with a song called "Garden Party." But his comeback was cut short when Rick died tragically in a plane crash in 1985 with six others in his party.

During my years at Imperial, what I really appreciated was the freedom to not only make decisions but to switch between my management role and creative interests at will. So it was with another Nelson, unrelated to Rick, that my creative side again rose to the surface. If you go on the Internet today and type in the name Sandy Nelson, several links will come up for the hit "Let There Be Drums." It's a song I titled and produced with Sandy Nelson soon after he signed with Imperial when he too was only a teenager.

Sandy Nelson was an unusual drummer. When we signed him, he already had a hit record called "Teen Beat," and like other young artists, it was on a small label and we were able to offer him a much better deal to sign with Imperial. He was the only teenage drummer in the country at the time that had had any success.

I came up with the title "Let There Be Drums" from the biblical story of creation. As I watched Sandy's hands and arms fly around the drum set with such confidence and force, I thought of thunder and lightning—the sound effects of creation. Interestingly, prior to titling the song, Sandy came to my office with the demo during one of Los Angeles's rare thunderstorms. As the demo played, the storm raged outside.

"Why don't we record the storm?" he suggested. So we put a microphone outside the window, recorded the storm, and added the sound to the initial version of the album. That was all part of coming up with the title. The single from the *Let There Be Drums* album became number two in the nation. It was the perfect thing for DJs to play late at night, and the album itself made it to the top five.

Sandy was a tremendous artist for us. After this first hit, we did concept albums where we covered different genres of music. One was a version of the top ten country hits of the time, or we'd cover R & B songs. It's interesting that most of his sales came from the Midwest, places like Chicago or Minneapolis, or in the West and Northeast. He didn't sell that much in the South.

I produced a live album with him in Las Vegas shortly before I left Imperial, and soon afterward three of his albums I had produced were in the national *Billboard* charts.

But Sandy's success was severely threatened when he had a terrible motorcycle accident and ended up losing a leg. Most people thought he'd never drum again. But he came back with the same force that he had originally, and the last I heard, he was still drumming.

When I think back on remarkable teenagers like Rick Nelson and Sandy Nelson, I can't help but contrast their lives to mine when I was a teenager in rural North Carolina.

CHAPTER TEN

LEAVING THE FOOTHILLS

The public library was off-limits to black children in my hometown of Franklin, North Carolina, which meant reading material was a prized commodity in the Ray household. Growing up, I read everything I could get my hands on. My mother would often bring popular magazines such as *Life*, *Reader's Digest*, and *The Saturday Evening Post* from the homes of wealthy white tourists where she sometimes worked. We also subscribed to the local *Franklin Press* newspaper and the paper from Asheville, North Carolina.

I was especially interested in what was happening in distant places, far from Franklin. Asheville was only about seventy miles from Franklin, but to me that was like in another world. We purchased most of our books from our local general store and from mail order catalogs.

Since my older sister, Annie Jean, had taught me how to read in my early childhood years, I was well prepared for learning at our segregated school called Macon County Consolidated School for Colored, located about fifteen minutes from our home. During my first few years, the school was housed in two dilapidated buildings without electricity or running water. Drinking water was drawn from an open well next to a cemetery, and heat was provided by coal-burning stoves in each room. The toilets were outhouses in a wooded area behind the school.

What the school lacked in supplies and facilities, it made up for in teachers—brilliant, dedicated teachers like Ms. Eula Kemp, my teacher for several grades. She was every young boy's dream—nice, very pretty, and took a real interest in each of her students, especially me since she was like a family friend, being a tenant in one of my father's rental houses. But it was my future education that she impacted the most, and she made sure I had extra assignments to prepare me for what may lie ahead. For instance, even though I couldn't go to the public library in town, she knew I'd use the library one day, so she taught me the Dewey decimal system.

When I was a young teen, Ms. Kemp would tell me about the excellent black high school she attended, a boarding school called Laurinburg Institute, in the eastern part of the state. My hometown school didn't go to the twelfth grade, so going away to complete high school wasn't unusual. My sister Annie Jean went to Allen Homes, a boarding high school for girls in Asheville, and my older brothers attended high schools in Asheboro and Black Mountain, North Carolina, but none of us had heard of Laurinburg Institute. However, based on the encouragement of Ms. Kemp, I decided that Laurinburg was where I wanted to go.

My parents, especially my mother, didn't object, seeing this as an opportunity for another child to leave the nest. What they didn't anticipate was what I decided to do the summer prior to going away to school—get a summer job that would take me far from the foothills of North Carolina.

The "Consolidated Tobacco Company Summer Youth Work Program" is what the advertisement said. I don't recall whether I saw it in a newspaper, a magazine, or a flyer, but I knew it was the best chance for me to make some money to help with my pending room and board at Laurinburg.

During the early 1940s, tobacco companies and other manufacturing plants had summer work programs targeted to youth, especially African-American youth in the South. I came across a similar advertisement for work at the cereal company Kellogg's in Battle Creek, Michigan. It didn't take me long to decide—actually it was no contest between the two. While I didn't relish the thought of working in the hot tobacco fields, Consolidated was located in Glastonbury, Connecticut, a suburb of Hartford, which I knew was close to New York City. Connecticut would put me close to the big city.

The day finally came when I was to leave home for the first time. I was sixteen years old, on my way to Connecticut for the summer. I felt a mixture of both excitement and fear. My father took me to the bus station at the town drug store in Franklin to catch the 6:00 p.m. bus to Asheville where I'd then take the nighttime train headed north.

Several years ago, I thought back to that pivotal point in my life and wrote prose that in part describes the experience:

I shall never forget the loneliness and sadness that I felt
Throughout that long, sleepless night
As I listened to the constant "click-clack"
of the railroad tracks,
And the lonesome, mourning whistle of my train

Slowly snaking up high mountains
And slithering down into deep valleys,
Carrying me away at only sixteen years of age
From the comfort and security of my loving family.

As the early morning sun arose above
a picturesque city skyline,
My tired old train "coasted" into Grand Central Station
In the big bustling city of NYC,
The first city that I had ever seen.

I found it interesting that when I got on the train in Asheville, I sat in the "colored only" section, but when the train reached Washington, DC, whites sat in my section. It was my first experience with integration.

When I reached Connecticut, I was pleasantly surprised at the living arrangements for us summer workers. The company grounds were like a college campus where we stayed in dorms, but instead of going to school we went into the fields. Consolidated Tobacco Company was the parent company of the popular Dutch Master Cigar Company. And I worked in the field for about a week before going into the curing house where I hung leaves and kept the fire going under the coal bricks. But having the opportunity to go to Hartford or New York as often as possible made the experience worth it.

Back home growing up, I had spent hours listening to the music of big bands like Glenn Miller, Duke Ellington, Artie Shaw, and Tommy Dorsey. That summer on the weekends, my friends and I would catch the bus to Hartford or New York to see many of those bands at the State Theatre in Hartford or the Apollo in Harlem. I can't say whether those three summer months created the foundation for my interest in the music business. If they did, I didn't know it at the time.

I do recall that while relaxing on a bench in Central Park, I daydreamed that one day something I created would be performed on Broadway or at the Apollo. Not that my own name would be in lights, but an artistic production that I had a part in doing would be displayed on the flashy billboards in Times Square. Amazingly, when I was just twenty-nine years old, those daydreams came true. I had produced hit records that were being played at the Apollo and in Greenwich Village, with the performing artists headlined on animated signs and billboards.

Following the summer in Connecticut, I went directly to Laurinburg Institute, as planned, for my senior year. What I didn't know then was that Laurinburg, founded in 1904, was one of the top African-American boarding high schools in the nation and today is the oldest of only four such boarding schools still remaining in the United States. It was started by Emmanuel McDuffie and his wife Tinny at the request of Booker T. Washington. When I was there, the McDuffies' son, Frank, headed the school. Since he had a PhD in economics, the curriculum for the senior class was designed for us to excel in business and economics.

One of our class projects was to run the campus store. I became store manager for a certain period where I did the buying, hiring, and firing, learned accounting and how to do profit and loss statements. It was certainly a unique experience for a high-schooler, one I'll never forget. I worked in the school cafeteria that year, but I stayed involved enough in activities to be voted class vice president. I also gladly took on extra assignments McDuffie would give me to keep me challenged, the way Ms. Kemp had, and I excelled academically to graduate second in my class.

Attending Laurinburg Institute those two semesters was the highlight of my teen years, but despite my achievements, I still graduated undecided about what I wanted to do with the rest of my life. I knew I had at least two options. I could follow my four older brothers and serve in the armed services. What they had accomplished made my family proud and was attractive to me. Our home mantle held metals of distinction for Mark, Milton, and Frank, who were World War II heroes, and Weldon received special recognition for helping build ships and planes that were vital to the war. My other option was to attend college, which I knew I'd eventually do, even if not right out of high school.

So I chose the army with a desire to attend officer's training school and hoping to eventually command a force of heroes like my brothers. It was an exciting dream that captured my imagination for weeks, especially after I passed the Army Specialized Training Reserve Program exam, or called ASTRP for short. That was the first step toward my special army career. I had taken the test before graduating from Laurinburg and, after returning to Hartford to work for the summer, received word that I had passed . That summer I wasn't at the tobacco plant but was hired at a ball bearing company.

The army notice said to report to Howard University in Washington, DC. Military programs were still segregated, so Howard was where African-American young men went. The program was challenging but enjoyable for me. We took classes in military sciences, geopolitics, foreign languages, and war weaponry and wore army reserve uniforms. I was at Howard for six months until I became eighteen years old and then went to Fort Bragg for several weeks of regular army basic training.

Following that, I had a choice to either continue studies in the Regular Army Specialized Training Program for a professional army career or go directly to Officers Candidate School (OCS). Of course I chose the OCS because it was part of my army plan. It was also a ninety-day program, and after graduation I would become an army second lieutenant. I was ready and my hopes were high.

But then disappointment struck. During the physical exam for Officers Candidate School, they discovered that cataracts were forming in my eyes and I couldn't pass the vision test. I was devastated. My dream of one day becoming a major army officer was cut off, just like that. There was nothing I could do. Army personnel told me I could continue my education as a civilian, and I received an honorable discharge. Most times I don't even mention that I served in the army, because my active service in the regular army totaled only 120 days.

The second option for my future came into full view. I planned to attend college in the fall, but first I returned to my job at the ball bearing company in Hartford. I had no idea where I'd go to college, but one day I said to my supervisor, "You know, I'll be going to MIT in the fall," thinking nothing of it. The next thing I knew, I was moved from the manufacturing side of the ball bearing plant, upstairs to what was called the "mic" room where I wore a white lab coat and used specific types of microscopes to make certain the measurement of each ball bearing was correct.

It wasn't MIT that I applied to but Delaware State University simply because I saw a picture of the beautiful campus and it looked like a nice place to go to school. At eighteen years of age, my decisions weren't the most rational, but when I was accepted by the college, I felt my life was back on course. That was until another advertisement caught my eye—*Schlitz, the Beer that*

Made Milwaukee Famous. Providence may have been at work again, because on a whim I decided to head to Milwaukee. To this day I can't explain it. I cancelled my application to Delaware State, hopped the train headed to Wisconsin, and ended up at Decca Records as a stock boy. It was the start of my sixty-year journey in the record business.

CHAPTER ELEVEN

THE ARRANGER

A fantastic musician and arranger. That's the only way I can describe Ernie Freeman, a man who could play any instrument, arrange any song, and create one-of-a-kind legendary hits.

Frank Sinatra's "Strangers in the Night" and Simon & Garfunkel's "Bridge Over Troubled Water" are two of the song legends for which Freeman won Grammy Awards for his arrangement. He even brought Dean Martin back into the limelight with "Everybody Loves Somebody." But Ernie Freeman was a talent I spotted long before his award-winning days of the 1960s and '70s.

When I first met him, he had a small jazz combo playing in a bar on West Adams Boulevard in Los Angeles in the early 1950s. At the time he was getting his master's degree in music from the University of Southern California.

Freeman started entertaining on the piano while in high school in Cleveland, Ohio, when he and his sister Evelyn formed a combo that became quite popular. After serving in World War II, he landed in Los Angeles and worked as a free-lance jazz, R & B and rock and roll pianist and arranger, which is why I tapped him to arrange "Hearts of Stone" in 1954. I paid attention to his career knowing it was only a matter of time before the world caught up with his talent.

In addition to freelancing, Freeman also recorded some of his own instrumentals, one of which began to sell nationally in the mid-1950s. Eventually I decided to bring him on our team at Imperial Records. We signed him to Imperial as an artist in 1957.

Freeman didn't leave his Cleveland fans behind when he headed for Los Angeles—at least they didn't leave him. One of his biggest fans was Cleveland's number one pop DJ, Bill Randle. I became acquainted with Randle during my travels to radio stations across the country. Randle loved Ernie, the rising star from his town. One day Randle called Lew Chudd.

"There's a perfect record for Ernie to do that's beginning to break in the East and the South. It's called 'Raunchy' by Bill Justis. It would be perfect for Ernie to cover."

Justis's record was on Sun, the same label that had broken Elvis Presley and a lot of other great artists out of Memphis. His record hadn't reached the West Coast yet, so I hadn't heard it. Randle airmailed it to me. I called Ernie who was on the road with The Platters and was in Portland, Oregon. I eventually reached him.

"Ernie, you've got to come record this thing."

"Eddie, there's no way. I'm on the road. I can't do it," Freeman responded firmly.

I wasn't deterred. "Look, when you finish tonight, I'll have a plane ticket for you at the airport. Go directly to the airport."

He finally acquiesced.

He flew from Portland to Los Angeles, arriving before eight o'clock the next morning. I picked him up at the airport and took him to my home. I played the record that Randle had sent. Without hesitation, Freeman turned to me and said, "This is a piece of crap! You've got to be kidding me. Where did you get this junk?"

"Never mind, Ernie," I calmly replied. "You've got to do it. It's going to be a smash hit. It's breaking. We've got no time."

Freeman sat there and listened to the record over and over again. Then he wrote the arrangement—just like that. But I knew he could do it on the spur of the moment with little time. That's why I had already scheduled studio time for ten o'clock that morning with Master Recorders on Fairfax Boulevard. I had also already called his buddies Plas Johnson, Earl Palmer, and other top studio musicians he always worked with. We went to the studio and recorded the song. Then I took him back to the airport, and he flew to Portland to join The Platters for their evening show.

In the meantime Bunny Robyne, Master Recorders' owner and chief engineer, rushed the original tape to the next step in the record-making process. Making a vinyl record, at least back then, was a multistep chemical bath process that usually took a minimum of twelve to eighteen hours or more to eventually produce a metal "stamper" from which records were pressed. Robyne was a first class engineer and had devised a method to cut the transfer time down to four to six hours. However, I couldn't wait even that long to start the record promotion, so I had Robyne record fifty "acetate lacquers" before I left the recording studio.

I first went to my former company, Central Record Sales. I was still pretty tight with the owner, Jim Warren. I played it for him along with the company's buyer, Mike Akapoff, a guy whom I had hired prior to my leaving.

"How many do you want me to take?" Warren asked.

"I want you to start with ten thousand," I replied.

"Ten thousand!" Jim exclaimed. "Why do we have to take so many? Can't we just buy a few to see how it does?"

"No, take ten thousand," I said confidently.

I also went next door to KFWB, the number one pop station in LA at the time, and played it for them. I told them about the original version by Bill Justis, "But there's no comparison between the two," I said. I got it as the pick hit of the week on that station. Naturally I took it to John Dolphin and some of my other radio contacts. Then I pulled strings to get the record pressing process speeded up at Monarch Pressing Plant on West Jefferson Boulevard through my buddy there, Nate Duroff.

So by three o'clock the next day, following Ernie Freeman first hearing "Raunchy," I had five thousand records shipped to Central Record Sales, half of their ten-thousand order. The planets must have been in alignment, because it was a remarkable feat on everybody's part.

In two weeks, Justis's version was number one in Baltimore, Maryland, but we were number one in Washington, DC. Justis was number one in Philadelphia and in New York. Ernie and I were number three in New York, but from Chicago west, we were number one—Chicago, Minneapolis, Seattle, LA. In the end, on the national charts, Justis was number one and we were number two—we sold almost one million of those records—not bad for what Freeman originally called junk.

Chatter on the Internet today still goes back and forth about which version is best.

I have fond memories of Freeman and was saddened to hear of his death in 1981, but I'm still in contact with his daughter, Janice, and incidentally, it was Freeman's sister, Evelyn, who recently said I "had an ear for what would sell." Evelyn was also a talented arranger and musician in her own right. When I hear her name, an interesting coincidence comes to mind. I can't help but think of my childhood when my mother and I would listen to two choirs on the radio on Sunday morning, one of which was the Wings Over Jordan Choir out of Cleveland. Evelyn, when she became of age, was one of the choir directors.

The other choir my mother and I would listen to was the Mormon Tabernacle Choir. Those Sunday mornings in my home in the small town of Franklin, North Carolina, are as vivid for me today as when I experienced them almost eighty years ago.

CHAPTER TWELVE

Stories from My Grandfather

The rectangular brown box with the big black knobs sat on the floor in the corner of our living room. I don't remember a time when we didn't have a radio. I do remember when we got indoor plumbing. I was around eleven years old. But the big Zenith radio was always there. We may have been among the first black families in our community to get one—either actually, running water or a radio. Little did I know as a young boy how important the latter would be in shaping my life.

However, I didn't have to think about the future much as a youngster. I was blessed to be born into a close knit two-parent home in a small, picturesque town situated at the foothills of the Great Smoky Mountains. Franklin, North Carolina was a resort community, where rich white families would come to their vacation homes in the winter to ski, or in the summer to fish in the crystal-clear mountain lakes and to enjoy the cool summer nights. The town looked like a photo in a travelogue brochure, a virtual Garden of Eden, and it's still known for gems used by jewelry makers and other artisans throughout the region.

I loved the natural beauty outside my childhood home. During the spring or summer, I could stand on the hillside and gaze in any direction and see mountains and valleys covered with blooming dogwoods, magnolias, and fields of wildflowers. But it was the warmth and beauty inside our four walls that's most seared into my memory—especially those Sunday mornings when my mother and I would listen to the Mormon Tabernacle Choir and the Wings Over Jordan on our radio.

My mother, Grace Ray, was the most important person in my life, the strongest thread in my life's tapestry. She built my self-esteem and almost went overboard in making her children feel more capable than anyone else, yet she taught us to value all people. She constantly reminded us, "You are the Rays. You are important and intelligent and do not have to follow the crowd." Then she would add, "However, be nice to everyone and respect their right to act as they choose."

No matter where my travels took me through the years, my first thought was always, *Mama, I wish you could see me now.* I was definitely my mother's son as a young boy. I looked like her, liked what she liked, and did whatever she wanted me to do, down to planting and tending the beautiful flowers and manicured shrubs that surrounded our two-story, four-bedroom home. I can still picture it. Our house was perched on a hill, painted white with bloodred trimming and topped off with a shiny tin roof.

There were eight of us siblings, nine counting an older brother Ernest, who died in childbirth. I was the seventh child, and for seven years had the coveted position of being the youngest, until two more sisters arrived. But I was still the youngest boy. Whether I was my mother's favorite, I can't say, but some of my brothers and sisters insist that I was. There was certainly enough love in our large brood to go around.

We had fun as a family. I can still smell the aroma of smoked barbecued ribs and the hot-buttered corn on the cob at our backyard family cookouts, and I enjoy reminiscing about my family gathered around the fireplace roasting peanuts and sweet potatoes while listening to the big-band sounds of Count Basie and Artie Shaw or the country twang of Roy Acuff and His Smoky Mountain Boys.

Our home was a safe haven—an oasis from the most despicable racist practices you could ever imagine that permeated our picturesque southern town. No, I didn't witness any lynchings, cross burnings, or bricks thrown through windows, but I was born into the "Jim Crow" era of separate eating places, separate drinking fountains, separate toilets, "black" and "white" textbooks for schools—separate and substandard everything. But despite these injustices, both my father and grandfather, through hard work and industrious minds, were able to create a livelihood that made the "Ray Clan" somewhat of a big fish in a little pond. It started with my grandfather, Matt Ray, a former slave.

I would sit fascinated at my grandfather's feet as he recounted stories of his childhood and how he ended up in Franklin. I was thankful that his stories were preserved in newspaper articles, written by local historian Margaret Siler who was able to interview him before he died. She also included him, along with other local "pioneers," some of whom were her relatives, in her 1938 book *Cherokee Indian Lore & Smoky Mountain Stories*. As I read those stories through the years, I'd smile to myself noting the difference between the "published version" and what he told us as children.

As a slave, Granddad belonged to Henry Ray who lived in Cane River Valley, near Asheville, North Carolina. When Henry died, everything that belonged to him, outside of his widow's dowry, had to be sold, including the slaves. Granddad, along with his twin brother and a sister, were lifted up on the auction block, but Mrs. Ray, the widow, was determined to keep them, so she bought them back.

"I remember hoeing corn when I was six years old, from sun up to sun down," Granddad would recount to us. He also remembered when he was set free and went to live with various aunts and uncles outside of Asheville. Then when he was sixteen, he would hire himself out doing various jobs. One of his first jobs was to take a pair of mules to Pickens County, Georgia. He made it there, stayed for well over a year, and went back to North Carolina. But the man he worked for in Georgia kept writing for him to come back. So without a means of transportation, Granddad set out on foot for a two-hundred-mile journey.

"I never got there," he recalled. "Franklin was as far as I got. My stiff, homemade boots had my feet so sore I had to stop here." In Franklin he ended up working for various farmers, one of whom was the postmaster who asked my grandfather to carry mail to the most remote mountain locations, a tortuous job others had tried and quit after only a few months.

"I carried that mail on mule back to Old Webster and other mountain areas for three winters and two summers! In the winter, it would be dark by the time I would get to the foot of Cowee Mountain. Lots of times Miss Mamie has gone out and thawed my shoes from the stirrups with a kettle of boiling water."

Granddad would tell us stories of his other ventures in Franklin and proudly said he was working with brick masons when "I handed the mason the first brick that was laid in the foundation of the courthouse that is standing there today." His stories were like movies to us children, and I let my imagination run wild.

My grandfather eventually became a landowner and gave land and helped construct a small chapel for blacks to worship in that was officially named Rays Chapel AME Zion Methodist Church. He was a popular man in town among blacks and whites, and with his savings he was able to acquire quite a few acres of farm land that also contained various fruit trees and forest land. Granddad became a major seller of fresh fruit and firewood. He later passed his desire for land ownership on to my father, Andrew Ray. Granddad and my father eventually built rental housing on some of the land they owned.

With the same entrepreneurial spirit as my grandfather, my father started a janitorial business in Franklin that was quite successful. He was a hard worker and would always say, "When you need a hand, look at the one at the end of your elbow." Sometimes he would take me with him to clean offices. I remember sitting behind big desks, my feet not even touching the floor, thinking, *One day I'm going to have a big desk in an office like this.*

My father became active in the community, although he was somewhat introverted. He chaired most of the important black community organizations and, despite his reserved personality, spoke out at meetings, effectively communicating his point of view to better the conditions of all residents. He, like my grandfather, was well respected inside and outside of our home.

Between the rental properties, janitorial business, and produce from my granddad's farm, the Rays became known as a
prominent black family in Franklin and we lived comfortably,
by the standards back then. However, we by no means lived in
luxury. All of the children worked, and my mother, who was
not enamored at all with the success of the Ray men, occasionally did domestic work at some of the rich white families'
private vacation homes. She was quite independent and wanted
her children to be so. She didn't even attend Rays Chapel on
Sunday, choosing instead to go to the black Episcopal church
on Roller Mills Road near our home.

Grace Ray seldom spoke of her childhood. She was reared
in abject poverty by a single mother, her father having died
when she was only three. Her mother was left to raise two little
babies, and among the family secrets is the story of her mother
taking Grace and her sister to a nearby river to end all three
of their lives. But before she could act, she believed she heard
the voice of God shouting at her to stop, that He would care
for the three of them.

Raising us was my mother's goal in life, where she found
joy, but that joy was not without heartbreak. My big sister
Annie Jean was unusually intelligent. She had a mind that
absorbed knowledge like a sponge, and she didn't hesitate to
impart that knowledge to her younger siblings. She taught me
how to read when I was four with books about black and white
heroes and magazines my mother would bring home. I would
spend hours with Annie Jean reading. She helped me develop
a love for learning that stayed with me the rest of my life.

Annie Jean attended an all-girls boarding school in Asheville and during summers and school vacation time would
babysit for a wealthy white family from New York City. They
too were impressed with her intelligence and encouraged

Annie Jean to go to New York with them and attend Columbia University, which she did. She would often send me postcards of the big city and write of the sights and sounds she was experiencing. But then something happened to Annie Jean's beautiful mind. I was still an adolescent and didn't understand what "nervous breakdown" meant, but I knew upon hearing the news that my parents were devastated. Annie Jean was in and out of mental hospitals the rest of her life, occasionally living with siblings, but never able to live again on her own.

Despite this tragedy my mother still wanted each of us to leave the nest, to leave Franklin when the time was right. She wanted us to experience the world, to set our sights high—higher than our small southern town. Sometimes I would see Mama sitting on the porch smoking, with a far-away look in her eye. I didn't know whether she was thinking about her poverty-stricken childhood and the contrast with her life now, or the tragedy of Annie Jean, or her dreams for her children to leave Franklin and see the world.

My father, on the other hand, would talk of us staying in Franklin to carry on the Ray legacy. While his aspirations for us were noble, my mother's dreams won out. We all eventually left, and after my parents died, we agreed to sell our land and the rental properties, each of us starting a new chapter.

My father, Andrew Ray.

My mother, Grace Ray. (1950s)

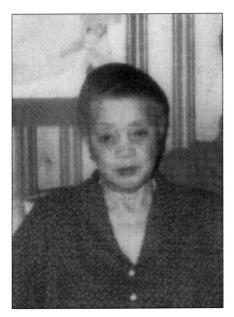

My sister Annie Jean Ray.

My brother Mark Ray.

My brother Milton and sister Nancy Jane Ray.

My brother Frank Ray. (Navy, World War II)

My sister Edith Washington.

Dick Ranta, Dean Department of Fine Arts & Communications, University of Memphis, at roasting reception upon my departure from Memphis.

Eddie Ray and Hall of Fame & Grammy Award Winner artist Al Green having fun at a Memphis radio station during late 1970s.

Eddie Ray, Hi Records' popular R & B artist Rufus Thomas, and Hi Records' A&R VP and Hall of Fame Grammy Award-winning producer-songwriter, Willie Mitchell.

With John Bakke, Dept. of Communications Chair, University of Memphis, and recording artist Ann People at the Governors Ball, Nashville, TN. (Early 1990s)

My wife, Joyce Ray, holding our baby son Michael Ray. (1967)

Eddie Ray with Grammy Award-winning artist Solomon Burke and
(far right) Gene Lucchesi, President of Sounds of Memphis. (mid-1970s)

Grammy Award-winning songwriter George Jackson and Eddie Ray. (Memphis, TN, 1975)

Eddie Ray with popular Hall of Fame recording artist Al Green. (Memphis, TN, mid-1970s)

Hall of Fame and Grammy Award-winning recording artist Lou Rawls and Eddie Ray reunite after having worked together at MGM Records in the 1970s. (Dallas, TX, late 1990s)

CHAPTER THIRTEEN

END OF THE ERA AT IMPERIAL

E ven though I was raised in the segregated South and was well acquainted with the overt messages of racism, traveling back there for a promotional trip was not high on Lew Chudd's agenda for me. "Under no circumstances do I want you going south," he stated emphatically. He didn't have to go into detail. No doubt because of being Jewish he was not immune to the sting of prejudice in the South and the North. Also, he knew the South would not accommodate his requirement that my travels be first class all the way from flight to hotel. "I don't want you segregated," he insisted. Like many he deemed segregation ridiculous and didn't want me subjected to it, at least not on company time.

But eventually I could no longer ignore the pleas of our southern distributors to pay them a visit, many of whom I'd met through the years at conventions in places like Atlantic

City, New York, and Chicago. So I convinced Lew that the South was still a place of business for me, despite its quest to hang onto racism.

On my first trip, I selected two cities, Miami and Atlanta. I picked Miami because I was unhappy with our sales in that market and I wanted to correct the problems we were having there. Another reason I chose Miami was because I had a positive coincidental history with a man named Henry Stone who had recently taken over the distributorship there. Stone was a former record producer at King Records in Cincinnati, Ohio, and had produced a hit record by the African-American group The Charms. That record was a cover of my song "Hearts of Stone." So I knew he was familiar with the potential sales of artists like those we had on Imperial and had successfully worked with many African-American artists and record promotion people. He was also aware that I was the cowriter of "Hearts of Stone" and in our telephone conversations praised my business accomplishments at Imperial.

Stone made the best reservations he could for me in Miami under the circumstances. He picked me up at the airport and took me to a hotel I'd read about in *Ebony* and *Jet* magazines, where all the black stars would hang out, a popular, plush place, but completely segregated. I stayed in Miami two nights and flew on to Atlanta to visit our largest distributor there, Southland. It was owned by Jake Friedman but run by Gwen Kessler.

I arrived in Atlanta late at night, and no one was there to pick me up because I had told Kessler I didn't know exactly when I would leave Miami and that I would get a cab to the hotel. When I went outside the Atlanta airport to get a cab, I was told I would have to get a black cab but an African-

American bellhop added, "All the colored cab drivers are gone for the night." Fortunately he asked me where I wanted to go.

"To the University Motel on the campus of Atlanta University," I replied.

"I'll be getting off in fifteen minutes and will be happy to drive you there," he said. Thanks to the kind bellhop, I arrived safely at the motel in the early morning hours.

I had chosen Atlanta not only because Southland was Imperial's number one distributor in the South but because I had new releases by Fats Domino, Ricky Nelson, and Slim Whitman and wanted to start our southern promotion for them there. I also had developed a successful working relationship with Kessler and wanted to cultivate it further with face-to-face contact.

The next morning a driver from Southland picked me up and took me to the record distributorship where I had breakfast with Kessler and her colleagues. After asking about my trip, Gwen apologized and said that I should have called her at home and she would have sent someone to pick me up from the airport regardless of the hour.

Southland's white promotions man and I started our rounds at various radio stations. As the noon hour approached while at a pop, Top 40 radio station on Georgia Tech's campus, I noticed an uncomfortable silence in the room. I immediately knew why, being the only black face in the group. *Would they relegate me, their special guest, to one of the segregated eateries while they went to lunch?* I wondered. It was one of those "elephant in the room" moments. Then the DJ finally spoke up.

"You know, there's a good deli downstairs. Why don't we order up some sandwiches and drinks. That way we can continue this interesting conversation." A silent sigh of relief echoed around the room, and I just smiled to myself admiring their work-around. We sat together eating sandwiches in the studio. "Ridiculous" was right.

Then not even six months later, segregation in public accommodations in the South ended. I immediately received a call from Kessler.

"Eddie, you have to come back. Please come back to Atlanta," she pleaded. So I went. This time she picked me up from the airport and took me to the Hyatt, one of Atlanta's finest hotels, and wined and dined me at exclusive French restaurants during my stay. Kessler just beamed at the dramatic change in her southern city. I was quite surprised, too.

By the early 1960s, big changes were also on the horizon for Imperial Record Manufacturing Company, although neither Lew Chudd nor I knew exactly how things would play out. I was still busy producing and selling hit records, and Chudd was busy building Imperial's catalog.

Chudd had recently purchased Minit Records, a label co-owned by Imperial's New Orleans distributor Joe Banashak along with one of the top R & B disc jockeys in New Orleans. Minit had begun selling records by their artists, but only in New Orleans. Chudd and I agreed that with our powerful network of distributors and strong radio contacts we could expand the New Orleans sales nationally.

In addition to several potential commercial artists, Minit Records had a young, brilliant musician, songwriter, and potential record producer named Allen Toussaint. Dave Bartholomew recognized Toussaint's talents early on and had begun employing him on some of Bartholomew's most important recording sessions, including some with Fats Domino.

Chudd kept the Minit label name, and shortly after acquiring it, Toussaint wrote and produced several national hits including "Mother-in-Law" recorded by Ernie K-Doe, "Ooh

Poo Pah Doo" by Jessie Hill, and "It Will Stand" by The Show-men along with regional hits by Irma Thomas and Aaron Nev-ille.

After leaving Minit Records in the early 1960s, Toussaint with a partner formed a successful production company and eventually built their own studio that attracted stars such as Paul McCartney and Paul Simon. Toussaint's songs have been covered by artists like the Rolling Stones, Al Hirt, and Glen Campbell. His many successes landed him in both the Rock and Roll and the Songwriters Hall of Fame.

Having a piece of the Toussaint pie early on was a real coup for Imperial Records, and it was a real pleasure for me to work so closely with such phenomenal musicians, songwrit-ers, and producers like Dave Bartholomew, Allen Toussaint, and Jimmy Haskell at Imperial, all of whom have become my lifelong friends.

The biggest change coming down the pike for Imperial in the early 1960s was in ownership. By then Chudd had built the company into an attractive enterprise. So now with both Fats Domino and Rick Nelson gone, and changes in the inde-pendent record industry in general, selling Imperial was in Chudd's sights. At the same time, leaving Imperial was in mine.

In 1963 Chudd sold Imperial to Liberty Records, whose parent company was Avnet Electronics. The whole operation was headed by Liberty's president and CEO Al Bennett. When Bennett took over Imperial, he begged me to stay, knowing I had one foot out the door. Even though I knew it was time to leave Imperial, I agreed to stay on for a few months, figur-ing I held the institutional memory and could help with the transition. However, looking back it was Providence at work again in my life.

In addition to Toussaint, another talented young artist Imperial acquired with the Minit label was rising, New Orleans R & B singer Irma Thomas. Bennett suggested that I bring Thomas to Hollywood to produce her with top studio musicians and expand her record sales potential, which at that point had been limited to the southern region. I brought Thomas to Hollywood for two weeks to give us a chance to know each other and to review hundreds of songs from popular West Coast songwriters. From them I was planning to select ten for her to record on an album.

Thomas was in her early twenties, and this was her first trip to California. She was definitely not a conversationalist, quite introverted, and probably homesick for her two young children back home in New Orleans. On numerous occasions during her visit, I asked her if she was a songwriter or had any original songs that we should consider for the recording session. Her answer was always, "No, sir." After I finally decided upon the ten songs, with no objections from Irma, I hired arranger H. B. Barnum to write the arrangements and set a recording date.

The night before the recording session, we had a little pre-recording party at Barnum's home in Hollywood Hills. During the party I noticed Ms. Thomas sitting alone at the piano, softly playing and singing. I went over and heard this one sentence of the song, "Sitting home alone, thinking about my past, wondering how I made it, wondering how long it's going to last." Noticing my presence, she stopped.

"Please keep singing, Irma," I encouraged.

Reluctantly she began again, this time with feeling and emotion I had never heard expressed by her before.

"Whose song is this, Irma?" I inquired with interest.

"Oh, this is just a little something I wrote," she quietly replied.

"But I've asked you—" I stopped in mid-sentence lest she feel chastised. I called H. B. over to listen.

After hearing one verse, Barnum said, "Eddie, I guess the party is over?"

"Yes," I replied.

"I have to go back to work?"

"Yes," I said.

"You have to have it for tomorrow morning's session?"

"You're damn right," I responded.

The song "Wish Someone Would Care" became a number one R & B national hit record, the first national hit that Thomas ever had. Three additional songs from that same album established her as an important pop and rock and roll artist as well.

Despite the success with Thomas, I finally told Bennett I had stayed much longer with Imperial than intended, that it was time for me to go, and that I had accepted a position with Capitol-Tower Records. He was willing to offer me almost three times what Capitol had offered to stay, but I told him it wasn't about money.

I knew Capitol-Tower would be a significant career move for me. I was going from the independent record industry to one of the major companies, the big leagues. Capitol Records with major stars like The Beatles, Nat King Cole, The Beach Boys, and a host of other top stars was consistently the number one or number two label in the nation, alternating positions with Columbia Records. Besides, my philosophy had always been that a person should plan to move when their career is on the upswing, before they reach the peak. That way they have more negotiating power with a potential new employer and can make better business decisions. Also, subconsciously their self-esteem will allow them to handle the unknowns of a new position with confidence.

I had almost reached the peak at Imperial. Ten years was a long time to be with one record company, one that was rapidly changing with some of their most popular artists now gone and a new owner. Fortunately, I was able to transition out just at the right time.

During my final days at Imperial, I began to reflect upon my successful ten-year run, the people I had met, friends I had made, and hit records I made happen. Of course I thought about my great working relationship with Lew Chudd, despite the dire predictions. I had to admit that both his business acumen and tough personality had rubbed off on me somewhat.

One day as I was packing up to leave, my mind strayed to a conversation Chudd and I had at our favorite Hollywood eatery down the street, Musso & Frank Grill. I pictured the eatery's walls lined with signed photographs of stars like Humphrey Bogart and Mickey Rooney. Writers F. Scott Fitzgerald, Orson Welles, and Ernest Hemingway had also been patrons. When Hollywood Boulevard declined into almost a skid-row street, Musso & Frank Grill remained. It was and still is a remnant of the boulevard's bygone glamour era, boasting today as Hollywood's oldest eatery.

But Chudd was in no way enamored with the Hollywood scene and always maintained a jaundiced eye toward it and the entertainment business we were in. His attitude would often spill over into our conversations at the restaurant. I recalled a piece of advice he gave me during a meal that served me well the rest of my record business career. I was sharing with him how pleased I was with our distributor in Philadelphia. It had not done much of anything with Imperial's products prior to my joining the company, but over a period of months, I worked them into one of our top distributorships.

I was relating to Chudd how the distributor, Nelson Verbit, and his wife would invite me to go to musicals with them and would have me over to their house for dinner and different events. Chudd looked at me between bites and said, "Yes, Eddie, as long as you've got hits they're going to be very nice to you. But remember one thing. When Rick Nelson stops selling, when Fats Domino stops selling, they're going to say, 'Eddie, do me a favor. Take your label across the street to another distributor.' There will be no more Broadway shows, no more personal invitations to the house." I discovered through the years that in numerous cases Chudd was right. His words toughened me, poured a little cement into my spine, which shielded me from surprise and disappointment.

"Mr. Ray, a young man is here to see you," my secretary said, snapping my mind back to the task at hand of tying up loose ends in my office before leaving Imperial.

"Does he have an appointment?"

"No, sir, he doesn't," she responded.

Now, my rule had always been not to see anyone without an appointment, but bending the rules, even my own sometimes, had been my *modus operandi.*

"Send him in," I heard myself saying.

The fresh-faced teen walked in and after a polite greeting asked if he could do an audition for me. Thinking he was about to give me a demo tape, I started to extend my hand until he went on to explain that he wanted to do it live.

Who in their right mind would do a live audition, I thought. *How risky is that?* He then proceeded to tell me every record I had produced, every company I had worked for, every hit record Imperial had. *Who is this teen?* I wondered in amazement.

Yet despite being duly impressed, I explained that I was about to leave Imperial and he could look me up once I got to Capitol-Tower.

"I will," he replied.

The young man's name was Mike Curb, and little did I know the impact he would have on my future. Barring my family, that young man turned out to be the longest, strongest, most colorful thread in my life's tapestry.

CHAPTER FOURTEEN

RIGHT PLACE AT THE RIGHT TIME

I saved Pink Floyd. I say that tongue-in-cheek, but I really did save the British rock group for Capitol Records, eventually resulting in their worldwide success on an American record label. The year was 1964 when I left Imperial to join a new division of Capitol Records in Hollywood called Tower. How I landed the position as A & R director at the record giant was a classic "right-place-at-the-right-time" moment for me.

Martoni's Italian Restaurant on Cahuenga Boulevard was a popular hangout for Hollywood record types. Like anglers bragging about catching "the big one," sales and promotions people would congregate around the bar after work, stretching the truth about their sales triumphs, unless of course the artist was present, in which case their sales tales would be much more down to earth. This was always a source of humor for me.

One evening I stopped by the restaurant to meet a friend, as I did occasionally since it was just a few blocks from Imperial.

As I walked back to the bar, I heard, "Hey, Eddie Ray." Sitting in a booth with another man was Ray Harris. For several years Harris had been a national sales representative for Capitol Records. He had recently resigned from Capitol to start his own independent record production company. Upon seeing him I immediately recalled how he had presented a couple of his new artists to me at Imperial whom I had turned down.

"Hi, Ray. How are things going with your new company?"

"Great, Eddie. I just placed one of my new artists with A & M Records." He quickly continued, "Eddie, have you heard that Capitol is starting a new subsidiary record label to be named Tower Records?"

"No," I answered.

He went on, "I understand that Capitol's president is looking for an A& R director for Tower who has experience working with independent record producers. With your background you should be perfect for that position. Would you be interested?"

"I don't know, but thanks for the information. I may check it out. Oh, I see my friend has arrived. Good seeing you, Ray, and good luck with your new production company," I said as I departed.

A few days later, I seriously mulled over my brief conversation with Harris and decided to follow up with Capitol on the new A & R position for two reasons—first, it was time for me to leave Imperial and second, I knew the significance of moving from an independent company to the record giant, not just for my career but for Capitol and the record industry in general.

I arranged an interview with Capitol President Alan Livingston. We had an interesting conversation about the major changes occurring in the record industry, but before I left, I said something to him I'll never forget.

"If I accept this position," I said, even though he hadn't even offered it to me yet. "If I accept this position, I insist on one thing. If I am to be hanged, it must be by my own hand," meaning I wanted complete autonomy to make decisions.

Two days later Livingston called. "Eddie, we'd like for you to become Capitol-Tower's new A & R director."

Despite Al Bennett's efforts to keep me on at Imperial, I accepted the Capitol position.

From that casual encounter at Martoni's with Ray Harris, it was impossible for me to anticipate the subsequent, successful five-year relationship I experienced with Capitol-Tower Records. And coincidently, once at Capitol I later acquired what became a national number one hit record on Tower, "Dirty Waters" by The Standells—from Ray Harris's independent production company.

Although Capitol Records came on the scene last among the nation's major record manufacturing companies, it climbed the ranks quickly with artists like Frank Sinatra, Judy Garland, Nat King Cole, Barbra Streisand, The Beach Boys, Lou Rawls, and Nancy Wilson, and country music superstars Tennessee Ernie Ford and Buck Owens. This meant Capitol continually vied with Columbia Records for the top spot among the four major companies.

Capitol's founders, Glenn Wallichs, Johnny Mercer, and Buddy DeSylva started the label in the early 1940s with Wallichs as board chairman, who took Capitol public within a few years. Wallichs wasn't a newcomer to the industry. He owned the largest record store in southern California called Music

City, located at the corner of Hollywood's famous Sunset and Vine. Music City was *the* music store for the Hollywood and Beverly Hills upper echelon.

By the early 1950s, Capitol's success attracted the British music giant EMI, which purchased the company in 1955. A year later the prominent Capitol building was opened, a tall cylindrical structure that remains a Hollywood landmark. In fact pictures of Hollywood Hills, with the famous sign, often include the thirteen-story Capitol building, dubbed Capitol Tower, peaking above the landscape. It was understood that Tower Records was named after the building.

British rock groups hit the shores of America in the early 1960s to appear on popular TV shows like *The Ed Sullivan Show* and *Hullabaloo*. The US record industry dubbed the influx the "British Invasion." Most of these groups were under contract with EMI, which by that time owned Capitol Records.

As a wholly-owned subsidiary of EMI, Capitol Records had first refusal rights for the US, Canada, and Mexico territories on all EMI recording products, including the British groups. But apparently EMI believed that Capitol's response to these British groups tended to be lukewarm and in some cases was a flat out "Thanks, but no thanks," allowing the groups to sign with competitive American labels. Interestingly even The Beatles, one of EMI's groups, had their first record release in America on a black-owned record label, Vee-Jay Records in Chicago, but some legal maneuvering quickly brought them back into Capitol's fold.

The primary purpose for creating the Tower Records division with its own staff was to give Capitol Records an opportunity to release more of EMI's British acts without overburdening Capitol's current A & R, and sales and distribution personnel as well as to prevent the British groups from going to competitive US companies.

However, there was another purpose for which Tower Records was created. Capitol was having the same problems that all the major record companies were experiencing. By the early 1960s, independent record manufacturers like Imperial had begun to eat into the total sales of the record giants—Capitol, Columbia, RCA, and Decca. Prior to this time, the independents accounted for a small percentage of record sales, so the major companies paid no attention to them. But when the independents started reaching 20, 30, and 40 percent of the nation's record sales, the majors took notice. Tower was going to be Capitol's answer to the independents—sort of a "if-you-can't-beat-'em-join-'em" strategy. So, all the records on the Tower label were going to be distributed through the strong independent distribution network instead of through Capitol's own distribution divisions.

The "British Invasion" was in full swing when I arrived at Capitol in 1964, and Capitol was struggling with its decisions regarding the signing of EMI's British groups. Shortly after I came on board, I read in a British music magazine that EMI artist Freddie & The Dreamers were coming to America to appear on ABC's *Shindig!* and NBC's *Hullabaloo.* I checked to see if Capitol had exercised its option to pick them up. They had and had already released the European hit single, "I'm Telling You Now." However, the song was a total flop and sold very few records on the Capitol label.

After I heard the record and checked our legal rights, I decided to rerelease it on the Tower label since the song sounded like a potential hit to me. I also believed that with the popularity of the two network TV shows and with Tower using the independent record distribution network it could sell.

I was right. As it turned out, the song "I'm Telling You Now" by Freddie & The Dreamers became Tower's first national number one hit.

Unfortunately, timing wasn't in our favor. Capitol had released the group right before the song took off. So, Freddie & The Dreamers signed with another American company, and Capitol didn't have enough other recordings by the group for Tower to follow the single with an album release.

Enter Pink Floyd. Soon after I joined Tower, the British group was becoming very popular in Europe. Again, I checked to see if Capitol was going to pick them up for the American market since they had first refusal rights. This time the answer was no. Apparently, Capitol had no intentions of picking up Pink Floyd, and less than two weeks remained on the option period before the group was free to sign with another US company.

Since one of the primary purposes of Tower was to handle British acts, I decided to investigate Pink Floyd's European popularity and review their recordings. The words *psychedelic*, *experimental*, and *innovation* kept turning up in reference to them. Upon hearing their recordings, I knew they were unlike any group that had yet hit America. I decided to exercise the option and signed them to Tower. I brought them to America for an album pre-release party and for local California media promotions. Tower released two albums by Pink Floyd, but unfortunately sales were only marginal. However, my decision to exercise Capitol's option and retain them saved the group for Capitol Records to share in the group's future, huge worldwide success.

"Hello, Eddie, this is Jerry Dennon from Seattle. I'm calling to congratulate you on your move to Capitol-Tower Records and to wish you the very best in your new position as A & R director."

"Thanks, Jerry, I appreciate your call and best wishes," I responded, pleased and surprised to hear from him. "How is everything going for you in the beautiful, great Northwest?" I asked.

"Everything is really going great for me. You probably heard that I started my own independent record distributorship in Seattle. I also formed my own record production company, and I've been fortunate to place a couple of my artists on Scepter and A & M Records that are beginning to show on the national charts."

"Wonderful news, Jerry. I'm happy to hear that things are going so well for you," I sincerely replied.

He continued. "Eddie, remember when I told you about 'Louie, Louie,' the record you missed?"

"Do I?! The memory is still too painful to discuss," I said half jokingly.

"Eddie, I recently released a record on my little label, and from the sales reactions we're getting from the initial airplay, it looks like a hit. I believe this could be your first hit on Tower because—"

"Jerry, send me a copy of the record today," I interrupted, "and I'll call you back immediately after I listen to it."

I purchased the record from Jerry Dennon. His production of "You Turn Me On" by Ian Whitcomb was Tower Records' second national number one hit, after "I'm Telling You Now."

But my early successes at Capitol-Tower didn't mean I had the golden touch with everyone I encountered. The "Louie,

Louie" story when I was with Imperial reminds me of some other major misses during my years at Capitol.

Big Brother and The Holding Company was a rock group that had two successful albums on a small record label. The group was free from its recording contract and was looking for a recording agreement with a larger company for worldwide distribution.

I went to San Francisco to see the group perform in the Haight Ashbury district at the Straight Theater. I was completely blown away by the performance of their female vocalist.

After the performance, I met with the group's manager at a coffee shop next door. We had a detailed discussion about the kind of deal they were looking for, and with the exception of a few minor points, I was confident we had a possible deal.

However, a few days after returning to my office, I was informed by our attorneys that some of the basic points I thought we had agreed upon had been changed. Nevertheless, I was confident we could resolve those issues and reach an agreement. But to my surprise shortly afterward, the group signed an agreement with Columbia Records. The female singer in that group was Janis Joplin.

Then an even bigger miss. One day I received a call from a man named Hillary Johnson, who worked for one of Capitol Records' distribution companies, this one in Chicago. I didn't know Johnson, but he knew of me and knew I was interested in independently produced music.

"Eddie, there's a new R & B group on a small record label that's begun to sell very well in the Chicago area. Their record is also on the charts of several R & B radio stations." He suggested that I come to Chicago and talk with the owners/managers of the group. I told him I was going to New York in a few days and would stop in Chicago. I asked him to arrange an appointment for me with the owner of the record. Johnson was able to set up the meeting and informed me that I could also see the group perform at a theater on the south side of Chicago.

Once in Chicago, I went to hear the group in a small theatre with only a handful of people in the audience. The young vocalist was sensational, and the group put on a good show despite the few people in the audience.

After the show, I met with the mother and father of the group and told them that I wanted to sign them to Capitol-Tower Records. The mother, a stunningly beautiful woman, sat quietly while the father did all the talking. We talked about a purchase price and distribution for the current record release; future singles and album recordings; royalty rates; court-approved minor contracts, etc. I felt extremely positive that we had a deal. The father said that there was one previous offer that he had to discuss and then he would call me with his final decision. I asked him to call as soon as possible because we didn't want to lose the radio exposure and sales that the group's current release was generating.

A few days later, the father called and said that he had made a deal with Motown Records. He said that Motown had agreed to put the group on a national TV show with another Motown star. Obviously, we could not make such a guarantee. So the group I lost to Motown was the Jackson Five with Michael Jackson!

Hillary Johnson later became vice president of national promotions for Atlantic Records, and a personal friend and he never stopped talking about how he and I lost Michael Jackson to Motown.

But signing future megastars or losing them to other record companies was all part of the record business, and it made my years at Capitol, as well as at Imperial, challenging and rewarding.

Capitol-Tower however, used much more than my ability to recognize talent early on. The company also relied upon my knowledge of and connections within the independent record distribution system. For instance I could easily bypass protocol and red tape and just pick up the phone and call my friend Gwen Kessler at Southland in Atlanta or Steve Poncio at United in Houston and get Tower's labels successfully distributed in their area.

Capitol's attorneys had limited experience negotiating and writing contracts with independent production companies. They had worked primarily with their own in-house A & R producers. I assisted them in developing many of Tower's independent producers' "lease-masters" agreements. These complex agreements would convey specified recording "masters" and exclusive artist's services to Tower Records, although the artists could still be signed to an independent production company.

I provided a whirlwind of education for Capitol-Tower management, attorneys, and sales executives. And that along with my success with the Tower label resulted in me being named vice president of Capitol-Tower Records, becoming the first African-American executive of a major record company. The year was 1965, a little over a year after joining the company.

When I think back on my success at Capitol-Tower Records, the positions I held, the artists I signed, the money I made for the company, one of my most memorable and unusual experiences was actually my first day on the job.

CHAPTER FIFTEEN

SPOTTING RARE TALENT

The words rang familiar to my ears. "Mr. Ray, a young man, Mike Curb, is here to see you." True to his word, young Mike Curb showed up at my door my first day at Capitol-Tower records. And true to my word, I agreed to see him, although I was shocked that he kept track of when I would start my new job and would actually show up my very first day.

We picked up where we left off at Imperial when he did a live audition. The seventeen-year-old had made quite an impression on me that day, not just because he knew everything about me and Imperial Records. A few minutes after I agreed to the live audition, the white teen, to my surprise, brought in three very attractive African-American young ladies as his group.

"You should have brought these ladies in at first, Mike. Maybe I would have been even more impressed," I later joked.

The ladies sang R & B/pop-oriented songs typical of what popular female groups were singing during the mid 1960s, and he had accompanied them on the keyboard. As I listened to him and the group that day at Imperial, I knew he had a rare talent, that he was something special. I soon found out that R & B was just one of his musical talents. In fact, there wasn't a genre of music he didn't know, and he had several different musical groups that performed at high school hops and college fraternities. Curb wrote the songs, managed their engagements, and accompanied them, singing and playing the keyboard—and again, he was only a teenager.

This day at Capitol-Tower, Curb hoped that I would sign some of his artists to Tower Records. My plans, however, already went beyond that. I was hoping to sign Curb himself as a fulltime producer with the conglomerate. Within several days I broached the idea with him thinking, *What teenager wouldn't be excited to join the top record company in the nation?* And of course he was. However, while the paperwork was being drawn up, I received a call.

"Hello, Mr. Ray. This is Mike Curb. I've been thinking about your offer to join Capitol-Tower, and I appreciate it very much and all that you're doing for me, but I've decided to continue on my own for a few years." As we talked, Curb indicated that he was going to give it around ten years on his own. Then I knew without a doubt that my instincts about him were right—this kid was going places, and his instincts about me as someone willing to help him were also right.

In my first encounters with Curb, my mind went back to Leo and Eddie Mesner who took me under their wing at Aladdin Records in Los Angeles when I wasn't much older than Curb. But unlike my uncertainty back then about my career, Curb was clear on where he was headed. He just needed the most direct route to get there—and he knew I had that knowledge.

Soon after our first meeting at Capitol-Tower, our bond was formed. One day Curb brought me a recording by one of his other teen groups, The Arrows, wanting me to pick it up for the Tower label.

"Mike, why don't you put it on your own label?" I encouraged. The thought had never dawned on him. "How do I do that?" he eagerly replied. I began to rehearse step-by-step how to create a record label, with one of the steps being to decide on a label name. The word *sidewalk* came to both of us almost immediately, sparked by his last name being Curb, so Sidewalk Records was his first label.

I suggested to Mike to press up about five hundred copies of the recording by The Arrows on Sidewalk Records and to initially release it only on the West Coast.

"I'll let you use my West Coast promotions man, George Sherlock," I said and then added, "But you must give Tower Records an option. If the record starts to make some noise, Tower will have first refusal rights to pick it up for national distribution."

Curb didn't know any record pressing plants, so I picked up the phone and called one of my cohorts. "I'm sending over a young man named Mike Curb, and I want you to press up about three hundred to five hundred records for him." I told Curb they would cost about ten cents each. Today Curb, a multimillionaire, unabashedly talks about that meeting with me.

"I started with nothing," he recalls. "I barely had enough money to buy five hundred presses. But sometimes if you have an idea and you believe in your idea, it isn't about money."

Once he and his sister Carole scraped up enough money for the records, we started promoting it on the West Coast.

As predicted, it started making some noise, so I picked it up for Tower Records. As it turned out, it was his first nationally charted record.

"The record was 'Apache '65,' by my group The Arrows," Curb recalls. "It was not only the first record on my Sidewalk label but also became my first *Billboard* charted record. This would never have happened without the belief of Eddie Ray. He subsequently signed my group. He also signed the three African-American ladies under the name The Starlets. You never forget the person who gave you your start," Curb adds.

"Apache '65" was a fast-paced instrumental featuring guitarist Davie Allan. Even to those who don't recognize the title, the song sounds familiar to listeners today, immediately bringing to mind the popular biker movies of the '60s.

It wasn't long before I discovered that Curb's business sense matched his musical talent. I don't know how he did it, but he had a way of convincing people, even me, to go along with his novel ideas, making all parties believe his proposal would be in their best interest. At times it was just sheer chutzpah. For example, still a teen, he approached the most successful independent movie production company in Hollywood, American International Pictures (AIP). Back then they were doing horror flicks starring actors like Bela Lugosi and other low-budget films that attracted teenagers. But in the mid-1960s, audience interest was quickly turning to beach movies and motorcycle films.

"Why don't you start making more of these kinds of movies," Curb told AIP producers, "and I'll do the music for you." He then went on with something like, "Look, I have a deal with Capitol-Tower Records that they have first refusal rights on every soundtrack I make for these pictures," intimating that Capitol-Tower was already on board with the idea. He suggested AIP could make additional money off the sale of the soundtracks, plus the soundtracks would be an additional promotional tool for the movie.

Curb then came to me with, "Eddie, I have a deal with AIP for seven movies, and I'll give you first refusal rights on them." He really didn't have anything final with either side, but he was confident that with the right negotiation and persuasion it would all work out. Actually it did work out, and in the end it became an excellent deal for everyone.

When Curb told me about the movie soundtracks that Capitol-Tower could purchase from him, I said, "How much? What are we talking about? What will be the price Capitol-Tower will have to pay for each album?" Curb suggested that I present a price proposal that I thought would be fair and profitable to each of us.

Sure, I was interested in deals that would make money for Capitol-Tower, but I also wanted a deal that would work for all parties. At the time Capitol Records was paying substantial amounts, maybe ten times more for movie and Broadway soundtracks than the final price we agreed upon. But of course these AIP soundtracks wouldn't be from major movies or Broadway musicals. Also these would be soundtracks by relatively unknown artists. So I agreed to pay him what I believed was reasonable.

The first two soundtracks we released sold over a half million albums, a stunning financial success for everyone. Curb was on his way to musical stardom, and I was on my way to the Capitol Records vice presidency, due in part to my early dealings with him. While I wasn't able to get Curb to join the company as a fulltime producer, I believe he did become Capitol's first independent producer.

Curb and I continued the soundtrack deal over a three-year period, and we must have had ten or so successfully selling albums from him, with a relatively small investment on Capitol-Tower's part. The albums included soundtracks from the 1966 hit *The Wild Angels*, starring Peter Fonda and Nancy Sinatra, and the music for the 1967 popular film *The Born Losers*. Today Curb has more than fifty motion picture soundtracks to his credit, has written more than four hundred songs, and has produced more than three hundred number one records, mostly in the country and gospel music arenas.

One of the vocal groups he formed while still in high school was called the Mike Curb Congregation, which years later ended up singing each week on the national TV show, *The Glen Campbell Goodtime Hour* on CBS.

Eventually Curb went on to head MGM, and I joined him later in my career. One day he came to me with a song he was thinking about recording with one of his MGM recording artists.

"What do you think, Eddie?" he asked after I heard the song. My reception was lukewarm, thinking it might be good for a Broadway musical, but not much more. Actually by this time it was already the title song to a kid's movie, and as Curb tells the story, "I put it out by The Mike Curb Congregation following the movie, and it was a bomb. It just didn't work. We even sang it on the Glen Campbell TV show and it was still a bomb. I was trying to figure out what to do."

Curb pitched it to his MGM company sales managers, the promotions VP, everyone, with the same negative response. We were all skeptical, especially when he proposed rerecording it with a particular artist.

As Curb recounts, "Sammy Davis Jr. had just signed with my record company and agreed to come to the studio to record the song, which he did—in one take. 'Sammy, would you try that again?' I asked. 'No,' Davis said, 'I just do one take.' So

I explained that I had made some recording mistakes and needed him to do certain parts over. So he sang just those parts and wouldn't sing the chorus again. My wife and I and a few others stayed at the studio all night trying to piece it together with the Congregation's background vocals."

That song was "The Candy Man" by Sammy Davis Jr., and it sold over 4.5 million copies, soaring to the number one song in the nation.

Curb's mile-high list of accomplishments and hit recording artists that he produced are phenomenal. He's received too many music industry awards to count, ranging from the prestigious Overall Producer of the Year Award from *Billboard* magazine in the early '70s to a star on the historic Hollywood Walk of Fame in recent years.

Remarkably my dealings with him at Capitol were only the beginning of our relationship. His words, "You never forget the person who gave you your start," were an understatement.

CHAPTER SIXTEEN

A STINT WITH TV PRODUCTION

T he idea came to me while lying in bed on a Sunday night. *Why not put together a premium album with three music legends—Dionne Warwick, Burt Bacharach, and Glen Campbell.* I chose these three because in 1969 they were top recording artists, had timeless mass appeal, and I had access to them.

I had just left Capitol Records to join a brand new television operation called Coburt Television Production Company in Beverly Hills. The name was a combination of its two founders, Pierre Cossette and Burt Sugarman. Sugarman was an investor whose wealthy family owned a number of businesses, including a cable operation and restaurant chains. He also owned a high-end auto imports dealership that kept him on the A-list of many stars. Sugarman was a young, handsome, rich Beverly Hills type, whose primary interests were business deals.

Pierre Cossette, on the other hand, had been a talent agent, a producer of a string of Broadway hits, and is credited with bringing the Grammy Awards to television. Actually he became the executive producer of the Grammy Awards Show for over thirty years. He was always cheerful and would have a new joke to tell every time he met you. In his autobiography, *Another Day in Showbiz: One Producer's Journey*, Cossette described Sugarman as a "tough, take-no-prisoners kind of businessman," and himself as just the opposite. That was pretty accurate, because Cossette showed little interest in the business side of the TV company but was totally engaged in the artistic and creative projects. He says he met Sugarman when Cossette sold him on the idea of putting up ten thousand dollars for an option on a book Cossette thought would make a great movie, but paid him back when Sugarman became nervous about the deal. Right after that they became partners in the television venture.

I was familiar with Cossette before joining Coburt because of the stars he handled through the years. But I didn't know of Sugarman until he called one day as I was nearing the end of my contract with Capitol, offering me a position and saying that I had been recommended. The offer sounded promising, and since I had already achieved a historic milestone at Capitol, moving on to a new arena was attractive. My philosophy, again, was to always leave a position when your career is still on the upswing.

So I decided not to renew my contract with Capitol and joined Coburt Company as the executive vice president of the new music division. My first task was to set up ASCAP and BMI publishing arms, which I did, allowing Coburt to publish original music and vignettes for their TV shows. And it was only a couple of weeks after joining the company that I had the idea for the premium album.

"How soon can you get the concept together?" Sugarman asked when I pitched it to him that Monday morning. I knew the company would want it by September, because that's when their TV special with the three artists would air and it would be an ideal venue to promote the album. But with this being July, we'd have to work fast.

The beauty of the premium album project was this: Coburt's upcoming TV show, starring Glen Campbell, with Dionne Warwick and Burt Bacharach, had a major sponsor, Chevrolet. That's because Sugarman was good friends with the vice president and general manager of the Chevy division, who happened to be the infamous John DeLorean. When DeLorean previously headed GM's Pontiac division, the automaker had sponsored one of Coburt's first shows, starring Ray Charles with the Los Angeles Philharmonic Orchestra, which was a big hit.

On the upcoming September show, the plan was to introduce Chevy's three new models. My idea was to feature the premium album on the show and offer it as a bonus gift for people who visited their local Chevy dealership. The show format would have Campbell and his guests Warwick and Bacharach gather around the piano, and Campbell would say something like, "Hey, Dionne, remember this song?" and they would sing part of one of her or Bacharach's hits. They'd then hold up the album, letting people know that the song and many others were on the new premium album and it was available as a promotional gift at their local Chevy dealership.

Sugarman, with his all-business-all-the-time manner, was immediately on board with the idea. So my first step was to secure the catalogs or older hits of the three artists. Glen Campbell's songs resided with Capitol, Warwick's with Scepter

Records, and Bacharach's with A & M Records. By Wednesday of that same week, I approached my former colleagues at Capitol and they went for the idea with some provisos. They would manufacture the album, including securing the contractual agreements from the other record companies, press the record, do all the shipping, handle the royalty payments—everything—for a fee, and they also wanted a guarantee of at least three hundred thousand albums. After some negotiating, I worked out the deal with Capitol that came to a little under a dollar per record.

I then asked Sugarman how much he thought we could get from Chevrolet to fund the project. We'd soon find out because by Thursday evening of that week he and I were on a plane to meet with DeLorean at the GM headquarters in Detroit. We stayed at a small exclusive hotel near the GM building and the next morning had breakfast in DeLorean's private dining room.

DeLorean loved the premium album idea, and we worked out a deal where Chevy dealerships would pay an amount considerably over a dollar per album, which would mean a reasonable profit for Coburt because of Coburt's small investment costs. The automaker's one stipulation was to have artistic control over the album cover that would feature the three new auto models to be introduced on the September TV special. It was a small concession for us, so we agreed, especially since I had already included pictures of the three models in my album concept.

DeLorean then took me to his team of vice presidents and other executives to roll out the plan. However, the negative vibes in the room were palpable. "There's no way we can do this!" "We don't want to be bothered with this now." "There's not enough time to pull it together by September." "No way!"

DeLorean summarily dismissed the mumbles of dissension by matter-of-factly stating, "I've already approved it."

So there I was, in the midst of all these corporate bigwigs, the only person of color in the room, and they all had to listen to my five-foot-something brown frame. I just smiled to myself at the irony. It was one of those personal, private triumphs.

Once back in Los Angeles, we started working on our part of the project, first touching base with the four regional GM dealership district managers who provided us with contact information for each Chevrolet dealership in the country. We then had to contact each dealership to find out how many albums they wanted for their customers, and I hired a bunch of students from UCLA to make the calls.

In the process I found out something interesting. The big dealerships in large cities were somewhat reluctant. They ordered maybe only twenty-five or fifty albums, but the small dealerships in "No-where's-ville" were excited to purchase the album with such big names, ordering five hundred or more and would often call back with a reorder within a week or less. Each evening we sent the orders to Capitol to be manufactured and shipped to each dealership. Every fifteen days we would submit invoices to each respective GM district manager for payment and would receive payment in full within thirty days.

The album was not only advertised on Coburt's September special but also on Glen Campbell's Sunday show and even on the TV hit *Bonanza*. In the end, the album sold 1.2 million copies in the US and another half million in Canada. All this took place in a month and a half—not bad for an idea that came about while lying in bed on a Sunday night.

After that success I returned to my music publishing duties and flew to Japan for ten days to set up Coburt's co-music publishing deals in Asia. Once back stateside, I began work on developing a record production company for Coburt. But I hadn't been with the TV company for even a year when I received a call.

"Eddie, I'd like for you and your wife to come to my house for dinner. I'll send my limousine for you."

We arrived at this beautiful home on one of the highest peaks in Beverly Hills. After a lovely dinner, he announced that he'd just been appointed president of MGM Records. It was Mike Curb, and he was in his twenties. Through a series of complex business deals, Curb had merged his various record operations with MGM, and the final agreement with company executives was that Curb join MGM Records as president.

He congratulated me on the Coburt album success and then said, "Why don't we talk about setting up a Coburt record distribution agreement with MGM," which we eventually did. Not long after that agreement was underway, Curb and I sat down to lunch.

"Eddie, listen, Eddie," Curb began. "You belong in the record business. What are you doing in TV production? You spend most of your time just providing music for their TV specials. You are a record man. I want you to join me at MGM," he urged in his persuasive manner.

"Mike, I'm under contract with Coburt. I can't just walk away." Curb then said he'd handle it, and a few days later he met with Sugarman. They worked out an amicable agreement. And so after only one year with Coburt, I joined MGM in 1970 as senior vice president of A & R Administration. I went to MGM primarily because of Mike Curb, who by that time had become a close personal friend. However, it ended up being a smart move because after only about two years, Coburt Television Production Company dissolved.

Working for MGM Records proved to be quite interesting, especially since Curb, as president, now had to report to a board of directors. For me MGM was challenging because as head of A & R Administration I was, among other things, responsible for licensing, legal, contract fulfillment, and I had to justify A & R expenditures by making several-million-dollar budget projections in such an unpredictable industry. But my years of experience and knack for predicting hits paid off.

In addition to Curb, MGM also had a very talented A & R director, a young man named Michael Lloyd, whom I had introduced to Curb when I had signed Lloyd to Tower Records.

Lloyd recalled that time in his early career and recounts:

> I was seventeen years old and signed to Tower Records. They were probably going to drop my band, but Eddie had always been supportive and didn't want to just toss me away. One day he asked me into his office and suggested that he set up a meeting with another young man, Mike Curb. Curb had a label (Sidewalk) distributed though Tower and maybe, under his guidance, I could develop further. I probably indicated that I didn't "need any help" but Eddie insisted, so I finally agreed.

> Now thirty-three years or so later, after millions of records, songs, awards, and wonderful times, I'm still joined at the hip with Mike. Eddie Ray's guidance in my life made all the difference. I can't contemplate what might have happened had Eddie not taken an interest and helped me…No matter what type of music or what type of artist, he's an equal opportunity dream maker!

We had a talented team at MGM, and during my four-year tenure with Curb, we produced hits such as "Spill the Wine" by Eric Burdon and War, The Osmonds' "One Bad Apple," of course "The Candy Man" by Sammy Davis Jr., and "Natural Man" by Lou Rawls.

One interesting side note about Lou Rawls joining MGM goes all the way back to my early days in Los Angeles at All Peoples Church and Community Center. The center, as I've mentioned, had a thriving sports program. A young man named Jimmy Tolbert was a very good athlete and active in the center's sports leagues. One day he told us he was going to go back to school, which he did and years later became one of the first black entertainment lawyers in Hollywood, and was the attorney for Lou Rawls. When Rawls was deciding to leave Capitol Records, he was approached by Mike Curb to join MGM. I was at MGM at the time. Rawls wasn't familiar with Curb, but I understand Tolbert told him about me and strongly suggested that he go with MGM, which he did. Mike Curb and Michael Lloyd ended up producing Rawls's Grammy Award-winning "Natural Man." That's just another example of how connections, no matter how seemingly minor at the time, are important.

We produced many other hits by such artists as Hank Williams Jr., the Mike Curb Congregation, and jazz organist Jimmy Smith, along with MGM movie soundtracks.

Our successful run at MGM eventually led to some interested buyers. Curb began company negotiations with the German engineering conglomerate Siemens, which purchased MGM in 1974. He left once the purchase was finalized to build his own company, Curb Records and the Curb/Warner label, taking a number of artists with him.

Siemens then planned to move the company headquarters to New York. I had no intentions of going to New York, so it was time for me to make a transition, too.

CHAPTER SEVENTEEN

FAREWELL CALIFORNIA

The sale of MGM Records to Siemens coincided with a mental shift for me in 1974. I was forty-eight years old and finally decided it was time to leave the employ of a record company, any record company. I had reached a point where I was no longer interested in being in sales and promotion, in A & R, or being a corporate mogul. It wasn't exactly a midlife crises or sudden revelation, just an acknowledgement, acceptance really, of thoughts that had been gnawing at me for a while.

I must do what I should have done when I was in my twenties at Central Record Sales and had formed R & B Records—develop my own record company and work for myself. That was my frame of mind in 1974. I didn't have any regrets about my career, but I had become preoccupied with musings about how far I might have taken my record label. I was certain, however, that given my knowledge, contacts, and experience, any business venture I pursued would be both satisfying and successful.

My attorney and I decided to set up Eddie Ray Music Enterprises as a corporate holding company where I could include any of my future music enterprises as wholly owned subsidiaries, including any music-oriented personal service activities of "Eddie Ray."

So when Motown called wanting me to join their Hollywood headquarters, I turned them down, as I did several other company offers. I couldn't be persuaded—except by one particular offer, but it still had to be on my terms.

Prior to MGM being sold, we had made a production deal with a company in Memphis called Sounds of Memphis Recording Studio, owned by the largest liquor distributors in the state of Tennessee, Gene Lucchesi and Paul Bomarito. They also owned hotels, One Stops, jukeboxes, and restaurants. In addition, the pair had a few big hits through their record production company, one of which was the iconic song "Wooly Bully" recorded in 1965 by Sam the Sham and The Pharaohs and distributed through MGM. I first became familiar with Lucchesi when I was at Capitol, having purchased a couple of records from his company, but got to know him on a more personal level once at MGM.

When I first visited with Lucchesi and Bomarito at their Sounds of Memphis operation, I was impressed by both the physical facilities and their artists and songwriters. During our conversations, Lucchesi would occasionally drop less-than-subtle-hints about "how wonderful it would be" for me to run the MGM/Sounds of Memphis production deal from his Memphis location. However, since he knew I was under contract exclusively with MGM, he never tried to hire me outright. That changed once the MGM sale to Siemens became public knowledge. One afternoon my phone rang.

"Hi, Eddie Ray, this is Gene Lucchesi from Memphis, and I'm out at the ranch. Paul and I are getting ready to go fishing and wish you were here to go with us."

"Hi, Gene, I'm not much of a fisherman," I replied, "but I'd like to just relax on that beautiful lake of yours."

Gene then got right to the point. "Eddie, we heard that you're leaving MGM, or are you going with Mike Curb?

"No, Gene, I haven't decided yet exactly what I want to do," and then I jokingly added, "But for your information, I will not be going fishing."

"Eddie," he interrupted, "Paul and I would like to fly out to LA to meet with you. We want you to come to Memphis and run all our music enterprises down here." He continued, "We're prepared to make you a great deal—a deal that you definitely cannot refuse."

"Gene, no offense, but that's what I am afraid of—I'm only kidding Gene!" In all seriousness, I continued, "It's OK for you and Paul to come and meet with me, but plan to come in about two weeks. By that time hopefully I will have decided what I'm going to do." I then firmly stressed, "As you can probably imagine, I'm getting several offers, but Gene I don't intend to ever work exclusively for one company for a salary again. So with that in mind, I will meet with you and Paul if you're still interested."

"Just tell us when we should come."

I made a deal with Lucchesi, agreeing to run Sounds of Memphis, but on a nonexclusive basis. In essence, he could contract with me through my new company, Eddie Ray Enterprises, leaving me free to pursue other ventures. I would also be part owner of Sounds of Memphis Recording Studios and hold one-half interest in a successful liquor store. He agreed to everything. It was a sweet deal for me once all the details were worked out. So like the song "Going to Kansas City," it was *Memphis here I come.* But I wouldn't go there alone.

⌇

"Have you lost your mind? You must be kidding! There is no way I'm going to live in that racist hellhole!" My wife, Joyce, was adamant. Memphis was not up for discussion with her. I saw the fire in her beautiful brown eyes when I broached the subject and knew I had to come up with a workable strategy.

Joyce and I had gotten married in 1966, almost two years after my first wife, Tessie, and I had divorced, and meeting Joyce was one of those unusual experiences. When Tessie and I parted just before I joined Capitol-Tower in 1964, I moved into a Hollywood hotel apartment located between Highland and LaBrea Avenue, two blocks north of the Roosevelt Hotel and Grauman's Chinese Theatre. That December the Tower Records staff had a holiday celebration at a restaurant in Hollywood Hills, not far from my apartment.

Tower's vice president of public relations, Perry Mayer, and his wife, Jane, invited their friend Evelyn to the party, who brought a guest, a very attractive Asian-American young lady of Chinese decent. She and I spent most of the evening together in a very enjoyable conversation.

Sometime during the evening, Mayer mentioned that he and his wife usually attended the opening day races at the Santa Anita Race Track on New Year's Day. They invited all of us to go with them. The Mayers said they would pick me up since I had just had my second eye operation and was unable to drive. Evelyn and her friend agreed to meet us at the track.

The Mayers and I arrived first. The first day of the races at Santa Anita was always a festive occasion, with thousands of people and a seemingly equal number of cars in the parking lots. We arrived about forty five minutes before the start, but Mayer had no problem parking because his parking space was part of his reserved ticket purchase.

With less than twenty minutes before the races began, I became a little concerned that the two young ladies that were to meet us there wouldn't show. But Mayer's wife, Jane, assured me they would be there because she had spoken to Evelyn earlier to confirm. About five minutes later, Evelyn finally arrived but without her Asian-American friend.

However, she had another extremely attractive young lady with her, this one African-American. Evelyn introduced her as her very good friend, Joyce Simmons.

After an exchange of greetings, Joyce sat beside me and quietly said, "I suppose you're surprised and disappointed that I am not your cute little Chinese lady."

"Surprised, maybe. Disappointed? Absolutely not, at least not at the moment," I replied.

"Don't expect it to get any better!" Joyce quipped.

I hope I have much more success and enjoyment with the races than with this smart a— My thoughts were immediately interrupted by the starting events on the track, which is where I focused my attention the remainder of the evening.

When the races ended, the ladies offered to drive me home since going through Hollywood would be convenient for them on their way to the Culver City area, more so than for the Mayers. On the ride to my apartment, Joyce sat in the back with me, and we had a reasonably pleasant conversation, mainly about the entertainment business. She shared a bit about her background.

"I'm from Muskogee, Oklahoma, and came to Los Angeles to go to college when I was eighteen," she explained. "The next year I met Harold Trenier, one of the brothers of the group, The Treniers." I nodded. I was very familiar with The Trenier Brothers, a very popular singing group in the early 1950s that headlined the Las Vegas, Atlantic City, Miami Beach, and Havana night club circuit. They also recorded on Columbia Records and had bit roles in several black-oriented movies of the early fifties.

She and Harold married, so she was accustomed to the entertainment lifestyle and did a little name-dropping of stars she had met. I listened attentively as she went on saying she and Harold had eventually divorced, that she had two children, a seven- and a three-year-old son, and she was twenty-nine years old.

"What's your phone number?" I asked as we neared my apartment.

"Why do you want my telephone number?" she quickly replied. "Don't you think a rather enjoyable day together at the races, where we both won a little money, is enough?"

"Perhaps you're right," I casually responded, "especially since you don't speak Chinese, or do you?" I could tell the barb surprised her.

"I didn't know you were a comedian too," she said.

"Well, if you give me your number, you'll learn more wonderful things about me." I was on a roll.

"Give me your card and I'll call you."

"Sorry," I said. "This was my day for relaxation, and I didn't bring any business cards with me. Anyway, it doesn't matter. As you said, we've had a nice day together." Then in a move that surprised me, she reached into her purse, took out her checkbook, took a check, and tore it in half. On the half with her address, she wrote her phone number.

During the next few months, we saw each other occasionally, and later in 1965 our courtship became serious. We married in early 1966.

Joyce was a gutsy woman, confident, and assertive—a good complement to me for many years. I recall a little incident shortly after our marriage that to me marked a significant difference between Joyce and my first wife, Tessie.

I was in New York with a couple of business associates, including a number of women. One of the women wanted to give me her phone number so I could contact her on my next trip to New York. I gave her my address book and asked her to write the information on the inner back cover. Apparently, she wrote her name and number in pencil. Several months later when I was in the city, I was checking my book for another number and noticed the inner back cover. The lady's name and number had been erased and replaced with the words, "What the hell are you looking for?" signed *Joyce*.

Another difference was that she welcomed involvement in my professional career, becoming like a partner, to the point of giving up an excellent position with the County of Los Angeles and taking a job as a reservation agent with United Airlines so that she, and sometimes the kids, could join me on some of my business trips, both domestic and abroad.

I'll never forget one business trip to New York. I came down on the elevator, and when the doors opened to the lobby, I looked in surprise and thought, *That woman looks a lot like Jo*—Before I finished the thought, I realized it was. She walked up to me and said, "You didn't think I was going to let you spend Thanksgiving alone in your hotel room did you?" *My kind of woman,* I thought.

Joyce was extremely bright and quick witted, however her aggressive spirit and sometimes sharp tongue were tempered by a deep-seated spiritually that increased through the years. She constantly said that neither she nor I had anything to do with us getting together, that God had sent me to her. To my surprise, she eventually told me in Memphis that she had decided to become an ordained minister.

But ministering in Memphis was far from her mind when I first told her we were going there. All she could think was I had lost my senses. In an attempt to calm her rant, I said, "What do you know about Memphis? Have you ever been there?"

"Hell no, and I don't intend to ever go. Besides, we have a beautiful home here in Woodland Hills where the boys go to excellent private schools, where there are no signs of dis-crimination."

"Honey," I interrupted, "there is racial prejudice and dis-crimination everywhere, so I don't think that should be the determining factor in making our decision."

She wasn't buying it and shot back, "For years now, I have supported you one hundred percent in whatever you wanted to do, but this time my answer is NO!"

"Well, we still have a little time, so we can discuss it later, but I'm telling you now, I will never work for any company just for a salary ever again!" I firmly stated.

"That's OK," she replied more calmly, "and if we ever need to, I will go back to work, but please, please, let's stay here in California," she pleaded.

Several similar conversations and arguments with Joyce failed to persuade me. My mind was made up, and in February 1974 I informed her that I had signed a nonexclusive agreement with Sounds of Memphis that included ownership interest in a million-dollar recording studio, a 50-percent partnership in a successful liquor store, and the right to operate my own Eddie

Ray Music Enterprises. This was an opportunity I couldn't refuse.

I suggested that she and the boys stay in California until the current school semester was over and then she could join me. She was absolutely shocked that I would make such a unilateral decision, but that tended to be my MO. I realized later that I added salt to the wound by purchasing a home and sending her photos of it afterward. Fortunately, she grew to love the home and eventually we both loved Memphis.

CHAPTER EIGHTEEN

HELLO, MEMPHIS

Memphis wasn't exactly the "racist hellhole" Joyce had predicted. Racist, yes, in many respects. But that wasn't unique to Memphis. As I had told her, racism and prejudice can be found anywhere. However it's not necessarily everywhere, at least when people get to know each other on a personal level, as in the case of Gene Lucchesi, Paul Bomarito, and me.

I drove to Memphis with the help of a friend, Dusty Rhodes, since my eye operations still limited my driving. On the way, we spent the night in Muskogee, Oklahoma, with Joyce's parents and arrived in Memphis the following afternoon. Rhodes and I went directly to the Travel Lodge on Airport Boulevard, where I would be living temporarily. We were warmly greeted by Lucchesi, Bomarito, and his brother Sam, who was co-owner/manager of the hotel and its popular Italian restaurant, where we all ate a late lunch.

Once settled in my hotel room, Paul took me downtown to meet the editor of the city's main newspaper, *The Memphis Press-Scimitar*. One of the paper's columnists, Bill Burk, interviewed me for his popular column "Good Evening Memphis," which appeared the next evening. I was also warmly welcomed by other media, including the top pop, country, and R & B radio stations. A few days later the southern regional editors for *Billboard* and *Cash Box* magazines contacted me for features, as well as several community newspapers. What a way to start my new venture in Memphis.

I poured myself into running Sounds of Memphis Recording Studio. For the first few weeks, I spent most of the day setting up my office, getting acquainted with the studio engineers, producers, writers, and artists. Most evenings I listened to Lucchesi's and Bomarito's colorful stories at some expensive restaurant, realizing how much Italians, at least these two, loved to eat and drink wine.

As the months passed, I spent time negotiating foreign subleasing agreements for the studio's publishing arm, renegotiating publisher BMI and ASCAP agreements, terminating old and negotiating new artists/record company production contracts, expanding the studio's custom service business, and working with the A & R staff.

But I knew even before arriving in Memphis that doing the usual day-to-day tasks, doing what was expected, would not be enough for me, especially now that I was operating under Eddie Ray Music Enterprises. In fact, as I walked into the state-of-the-art studio each morning, an opportunity began to gel in my mind that I knew would turn the "usual" upside down. The courage to "break the rules" began to rise within.

This would be an ideal place for a vocational commercial music school, was the thought that began to form. *We have the space, equipment, technical people, experience, and knowledge right here.* I knew of one other vocational music school in the country, The San Francisco College for Recording Arts, operated by Leo De Gar Kulka. He was a professor at California State University at San Francisco and also owned Golden State Recorders, Inc., which housed the school. I had been a guest lecturer on a couple of occasions there. *All we need are the necessary approvals to do something similar here in Memphis,* I thought.

But despite my courage to forge ahead with the school idea and Lucchesi being able to connect me with some key people, getting the required authorization to start a commercial music school proved to be a more daunting task than I had imagined. I went back and forth to this board and that agency. Votes were taken, dozens of meetings, contracts, discussions, and decisions occurred.

Compounding the long, drawn-out process wasn't the racial discrimination toward me that I had anticipated. Something else was at play that I wasn't expecting—the infamous, invisible "Southern Stonewall," meant to stop "outsiders" in their tracks, skin color notwithstanding. It was fully erected in Memphis. The underlying current was almost audible. "Who is this guy from Hollywood coming here thinking he's going to change things? Who does he think he is?"

But brick by brick I dismantled the wall until there was nothing left except a clear path of support for what I was attempting to do. Lucchesi was one of my biggest supporters, agreeing to allow me to use the studio for the school at no charge until the project was profitable and then pay whatever I decided was fair. Once the final green light was on from the Tennessee State Secondary Education Department, I first formed a nonprofit organization, the Tennessee College for Recording Arts, Inc., which would own and operate the school.

In the spring of 1975, the College for Recording Arts opened in the Sounds of Memphis Recording Studio at 904 Rayner Street. It was one of my proudest achievements because within a little over a year, I had pulled together the resources necessary to create a significant institution from scratch—a feat many said could not be done. But that wasn't my motivation for insisting upon the school. I knew from experience in Memphis that despite the almost glut of talented musical artists, there was a dearth of people who knew about the management, production, and operations side of the industry. People were being hired who knew nothing about music publishing, BMI and ASCAP, and artist contracts. Record companies had to go outside of Memphis and bring people in from New York, Los Angeles, or Nashville for certain roles.

I wanted the school to develop local young people to assume these positions, especially African-American young people. I envisioned them flocking to the studio, wanting to learn all aspects of the music business. However, as it turned out, 95 percent of my students were white, primarily because of the tuition cost.

I put together a strong board of directors for the school, including, of course, Leo De Gar Kulka, as well as one of his colleagues from his San Francisco school, Herbert Hass. Martin Berlanstein, a Memphis attorney, was also a board member. He was one of only a couple of entertainment attorneys in town and had also served at the Federal Trade Commission in Washington, DC. My wife, Joyce, was the college registrar as well as a board member. I had the title of president of the Tennessee College for Recording Arts, Inc. and dean of the College for Recording Arts.

The curriculum was designed to give students broad training in the music industry. As I wrote in the college bulletin, "A music industry leader...needs to know musicianship, without necessarily being a musician; must understand sound engineering, without needing to be an expert mixer; must have a grasp of law and finance, without needing to be a lawyer or accountant."

I made sure the courses were comprehensive, taught by active industry professionals. We had beginning and advanced courses in audio engineering, music production, law, and the business and finance side of the music industry. I would occasionally take students with me on trips to New York or Los Angeles to visit major record companies and meet industry leaders, and I would often bring in guest speakers, buddies of mine who were as enthusiastic about the school as I was.

The program consisted of three quarters of fourteen weeks each, with an optional fourth quarter in Record Company Operation, and students completing the program received a diploma. The school was a tremendous success with approximately ninety students graduating in the first class.

My years in Memphis proved to be quite significant for me in other ways. While my vocational students soaked up the hands-on practical education of the commercial music industry, my own educational quest rested on the opposite end of the spectrum. I sought more theory and the academics that would result in obtaining a bachelor's degree. I had taken a few courses toward a BA while still in California, but now I no longer wanted to place continuing my education on the back burner.

On several occasions I had met professors from Memphis State University—as it was known then and years later renamed University of Memphis—who told me, "You know, with the advanced college courses you've already taken and your professional experience, it shouldn't take that many hours for you to get your BA."

So, pushing fifty years old, I enrolled at Memphis State to pursue a degree in communications. I knew many of my classmates would be less than half my age, and while some in middle age might find that fact unsettling, I relished the thought of sharing my insights with those interested. To my delight, my classmates as well as my professors were interested. I actually became a popular student. I led group projects, had groups gather around me after class to hear my stories about the record business, went to the local watering hole with professors, and basically had one of the most enjoyable periods of my life.

One of my communications professors, Dr. John Bakke, who remains a lifelong friend, recently wrote a tribute to me that I treasure because it's one of the reminders of such a fulfilling time:

> Eddie always seemed to be on the edge of his chair for all three hours of the once-a-week class. His eyes were always wide open, his face always seemed to respond appropriately, and his hand was always going up when he had something to ask about or say when his participation was relevant and helpful to himself and the class. I must add here that Eddie Ray never did anything to "throw his experience around" or show off in any way. Whenever he took issue with what was being said or presented, it was always with openness and respect. If I had more students like Eddie Ray, I might still be teaching. The "A" he earned in the course through his participation, exams, and papers did not do him justice. He was really a colleague who was above the normal

system of evaluation used for normal students, even the outstanding normal ones.

I received my BA degree in 1978.

Memphis State University played an important role in the future of the vocational school. I closed the physical location of the school at Sounds of Memphis after only two years because a significant number of prospective students could not afford the tuition costs without grants or other financial help that the school was unable to provide. However, the school concept was able to live on, having been adopted by Memphis State University's Department of Communication.

It was another proud moment for me when I was successful in convincing university officials to accept and develop the curriculum into a commercial music degree program. Again I wanted African-American young people to enroll at the university to get a degree, but in addition to the finances being a barrier, to my disappointment, many were not interested in the courses required for a degree, courses not directly tied to the music business. So the commercial music degree program at Memphis State University that I had initiated ended up being comprised of 90 percent European-American students at that time.

Memphis held some other disappointments for me—but not before a few surprises, the first of which would add to my already busy schedule and significantly increase my income. I picked up the phone one day in my Sounds of Memphis office and heard a familiar voice.

"Eddie, this is Al Bennett. Perhaps you've heard that my company has bought Hi Records and the East Memphis Music Publishing Company. I'll be in Memphis next week and want to meet with you to discuss the possibility of you running both companies for us."

CHAPTER NINETEEN

Connections and Reconnections

Your past catches up with you is an axiom that became literal in my case in Memphis, but in a very positive sense.

Upon hearing Al Bennett's voice, my mind immediately went back to 1963 when Bennett tried his best to keep me at Imperial Records after he purchased the company from Lew Chudd. Since then I had heard Bennett had been successful buying up independent record companies, which was the reason for this call. He explained that he had recently purchased Hi Records in Memphis along with East Memphis Music Publishing Company and he wanted me to run both.

I didn't want to turn him down again, but I explained, "Al, thank you for the offer, but I must tell you that if I do this, it has to be on a nonexclusive basis because I have my own company now, Eddie Ray Music Enterprises. I contract my services, which is what I'm doing with Sounds of Memphis."

Bennett indicated that a contractual arrangement with me would be no problem. So in May, 1977, I became vice president and general manager of Cream/Hi Records and East Memphis Music Publishing Company, adding to my Sounds of Memphis duties. Hi Records, which by that time Bennett had renamed Cream/Hi Records, was noted in the early '70s for having the popular R & B artist Al Green.

In 1969 Green met Hi Records Vice President Willie Mitchell who signed him to the label and collaborated with Green on early 1970s hits such as "Let's Stay Together," "Tired of Being Alone," "I'm Still in Love With You," and "Call Me." But according to news reports, at the height of his popularity, Green's former girlfriend broke into his Memphis home in October 1974 and poured boiling grits on the singer as he was bathing, inflicting second-degree burns on his back, stomach, and arm. After that incident, Green entered the ministry and purchased a church in Memphis, which I attended many times.

Another acquaintance who surfaced was Sam Trust. I met him at Capitol when he joined the company as president of the publishing division. We worked closely together, but he left Capitol before me to take a primo position as the international president of the giant English music publishing company, ATV, that held most of The Beatles' most popular song copyrights. There he formed joint ventures with small independent American and European publishing firms, which is why he contacted me in Memphis.

Trust was interested in a deal involving my ASCAP and BMI music publishing companies that were subsidiaries of Eddie Ray Music Enterprises. I liked what Trust proposed, so we entered into a joint venture, which meant a substantial advance for me from ATV. Incidentally, ATV made international headlines much later when it was purchased by Michael Jackson before being merged into Sony/ATV Music Publishing—but I was too far removed from those deals and had only a few copyrights remaining in their catalog to see any additional financial benefit.

Bennett and Trust were not the only reconnections I made in Memphis. Shortly after arriving, I received a call from a longtime friend, Chuck Scruggs, whom I first met back in 1955 after joining Imperial Records. Back then Scruggs was an afternoon drive-time DJ at station WCIN in Cincinnati. But when he called me in Memphis in 1974, after seeing the *Memphis Press-Scimitar* article about my arrival, he was executive vice president and general manager of WDIA, one of the top R & B stations in Memphis as well as the nation. Most recently Scruggs was a popular TV host of a children's show at WKNO-TV in Tennessee called *Hello Mr. Chuck*.

The warmth of his good-natured personality endears him to his young TV audience as it has to me through the years. And unbeknownst to me when we first became acquainted back in the mid-1950s, something about my personality clicked with him as he recalls today:

> Eddie serviced our station (WCIN in Cincinnati) personally with the latest R & B records. What would later become known as "soul music" was impacting record sales from one end of the country to the other. Eddie was soon to become known as one of the industry's most effective record promoters. He was well respected, even by his peers. For many of us broadcasters, Eddie was regarded as "Mister Congeniality," mostly because

of his consistent, cool, confident, laid-back approach to what could be a stressful industry. Eddie secured the necessary air-play, not only because he usually had good product but because he was a straight shooter. He didn't use a lot of hype.

Scruggs is another long, strong thread in my life's tapestry, and the mutual admiration society we formed as colleagues spilled over into a personal friendship that includes family outings, even family vacations. A few weeks after my arrival in Memphis, Scruggs and his wife, Jean, had a party for me in their home to meet some of the city's African-American VIPs.

Actually, Memphis is where I met some of the most interesting people of my career, people who would have an impact on my future both personally and professionally.

"I first saw Eddie right after I signed a recording contract with Cream/Hi Records. He was sitting in his office and had on a midnight navy suit, light blue shirt with a white collar and cuffs, and had on tinted glasses contrasting with his silver white hair. I said to the person with me, 'Whoever that guy is, I want to meet him. That's the guy I want to meet.' Sometime later his secretary called and said, 'Mr. Ray would like to meet with you.' 'Are you serious?' I said. I didn't realize at the time the impact Eddie would have on my life."

That's how Larry "T-Byrd" Gordon remembered our first encounter. He and his band were artists from Dallas, Texas, and Cream/Hi's Willie Mitchell had signed and recorded one session with them. Mitchell gave me the demos, and I was more interested in T-Byrd's saxophone performance than in the group or in the particular song they recorded. Later I called Bennett in Los Angeles and told him how impressed I was with T-Byrd, and he suggested that I bring him to Los

Angeles to record with my musicians there. I then asked my secretary to invite the talented musician to lunch before he went back to Dallas. That one lunch meeting was the start of a friendship that lasted until T-Byrd's untimely death in late April 2011.

"Eddie helped me and my wife, Carrie, develop a record label, LaMé Records, helped us form a corporation, and is even my son's godfather. He has been a father to me. I love him dearly," Gordon said not long before he succumbed to heart failure. With a PhD he taught humanities at a college in Texas. His band was popular throughout the Southwest, West Coast, Monte Carlo, and major European countries, performing at corporate and private country clubs and other high society events. His extraordinary gift on the saxophone began when he started playing in the fifth grade. Remarkably, T-Byrd Gordon played twenty-seven instruments—one of those rare talents I had the privilege of spotting early on. His wife, Carrie, is the mayor of their town, Balch Springs, Texas, and their son Larry II, my godson, whom I comanage, is a rising songwriter and recording star.

I met another interesting young man in Memphis, this one through Chuck Scruggs. Scruggs had hired Michael Frisby as music director at his station, WDIA, and after only two years at the station, Frisby was selected as the number one R & B music director in the nation by a *Billboard* magazine poll. But one day, I found out that despite his success, Frisby's heart was no longer in radio.

"I'm thinking about leaving the radio broadcast business to become an entertainment attorney," he told me at lunch one day, catching me by surprise.

"Well, Michael, you know you'll have to attend law school, and chances of building a successful entertainment law practice in Memphis will be extremely difficult," I counseled cautiously, not wanting to discourage him, but I had to be realistic.

Then the shocker. Frisby said, "I've already graduated from Harvard Law School—ranked in the top percent of my class. While at Harvard I was a DJ on a local Boston R & B station and became hooked on radio broadcasting."

Once I regrouped from the surprise, I suggested that Frisby let me send his resume to a few entertainment law firm contacts in Hollywood and Beverly Hills, which I did.

I soon received a call from my friend Joel Strote, an attorney with the Beverly Hills Strote & Straw Law Firm, asking me to arrange an interview with Frisby because he was so impressed with his credentials. Frisby met with Strote and, after giving WDIA notice, joined the law firm, successfully passing the California Bar, and started working with the firm's many movie and music clients. Today Frisby is vice president and assistant general counsel at Sony Pictures Entertainment. Before his rise to this prominent post, however, I would reconnect with Frisby in an interesting way once I returned to California

Memphis sparked a long line of acquaintances, friends, business associates, and memories that I carry in my heart and mind to this day. I remember being in Memphis when the city became the spotlight of the world with the death of Elvis Presley in 1977. The outpouring of emotion was akin to the assassination of President John F. Kennedy. Signs and shrines lined the streets everywhere. Whether people worshipped him or held a jaded eye believing he garnered more credit than deserved for the initiation of the rock and roll era, they all agreed that Presley made a significant impact on the music industry during a time of major transition.

I never met Presley, however for several years on the anniversary of his death, Dr. Bakke had me return to the University of Memphis to participate in a day-long celebration of Elvis's life and legacy.

I often think back to Gene Lucchesi, responsible for starting my Memphis experience with that phone call back in 1974 when I was about to leave MGM. But even more memorable was the call I received from him more than thirty years later.

"Eddie, this is Gene. I'm just calling to say good-bye."

"What are you talking about Gene? Where are you going? You're not going anywhere."

"I just called to say good-bye, Eddie," he repeated, barely audible. I found out that just two hours after the call Lucchesi died of natural causes, with his daughter Linda by his side.

"My father always said Eddie was like his own brother, and he wanted to talk to him before he died." Linda Lucchesi and I continue to be good friends. She relied on me for music advice through the years once she purchased Sounds of Memphis in the mid-1980s, but our real bond was rooted in my relationship with her remarkable father.

Sadly one important relationship that I would not carry with me when I left Memphis was with my wife Joyce. As she embraced Memphis and Memphis embraced her, our interests diverged. Her spiritual life grew exponentially, and my professional life was consuming. She decided to go to school to study the ministry, and when she announced that she was going to become an ordained minister, I didn't share her enthusiasm nor offer the level of support she gave me in my career ventures. Our schedules eventually made it impossible to spend as much time together as we had when we came to Memphis. So when I said I was thinking about returning to California to pursue another dream, it was too much for her.

I left Memphis in July of 1979. Joyce and I had divorced earlier that year. She went on to become a minister of a multimillion-dollar megachurch complex. We did maintain a cordial relationship, in part because of our boys, Tracy and Michael, and I would sometimes visit her church when in Memphis. She died on November 6, 2003, and I attended her huge funeral. Just a few years ago I visited her gravesite and thanked her for thirteen wonderful years together.

California Lt. Governor Mike Curb and Eddie Ray endure frigid weather during inaugural festivities of President Ronald Reagan. (Washington, DC, 1981)

President Ronald Reagan and US Commissioner Eddie Ray at the White House. (Washington, DC, early 1980s)

US Commissioner, Chairman Eddie Ray on the front cover of *Mainstream America* magazine. (Washington, DC, 1985)

Baseball Commissioner Bowie Kuhn testifying before Chairman Eddie Ray and the US Copyright Royalty Tribunal. (Washington, DC, mid-1980s)

Farewell reception upon my retirement from the US Copyright Royalty Tribunal. (Washington, DC, 1989)

Larry "T-Byrd" Gordon (second from left), Carrie Gordon, Eddie Ray, and "T-Byrd's" band arranger, East Berlin, Germany. (Late 1990s)

Eddie Ray and wife Jeanette at the North Carolina Music Hall of Fame Induction Ceremony. (Kannapolis, NC, 2009)

Eddie Ray reunited with attorney Michael Frisby, VP General Counsel, Columbia-Sony Pictures, after having worked together in Memphis, TN in the 1970s. (Culver City, CA, 2009)

Eddie Ray and wife Jeanette with Barbara Hall, coauthor, and husband Michael Hall at Eddie Ray's North Carolina Music Hall of Fame Induction. (Kannapolis, NC, October 2009)

Mike Curb and Eddie Ray during Eddie Ray's induction into the North Carolina Music Hall of Fame. (Kannapolis, NC, October 2009)

CHAPTER TWENTY

OUT OF THE BOX

mazing what you can create from nothing. APAC—
Alternative Political Action Committee—was one
of the hottest little political groups in Los Angeles
in 1980, and I created it out of thin air, just to keep the pot
stirred. The committee was a group of thirteen African-
American professionals who yielded their time and influence
to get Ronald Reagan elected president. APAC was probably
the most out-of-the-box, pushing-the-envelope move of my
career. However, becoming involved in politics wasn't my
initial idea. In fact, it was the furthest thought from my mind
as I prepared to leave Memphis.

When I decided to leave the city in 1979 and return to
California, the media was right there to record my departure
as it had been to herald my arrival. In Bill Burk's August 22,

1979 "Good Evening Memphis" column in *The Memphis Press-Scimitar*, he wrote:

> Seldom has a newcomer to any city contributed as much to his new home as Eddie Ray since he moved from Los Angeles to the Bluff City in 1974. Ray arrived as executive vice president of Sounds of Memphis, Inc. In the interim, the highly likable executive has become a trustee of the National Academy of Recording Arts and Sciences; a member of the board of governors of Country Music, Memphis Style; a member of Memphis State University's Music Advisory Board; and executive vice president and general manager of Cream/Hi Records. He founded the Tennessee College of Recording Arts and Sciences, and set up Eddie Ray Music Enterprises... It's going to be awfully hard to see Eddie Ray leave. He's going to leave a pair of size 20 EEE shoes to fill and I'm not sure Al Bennett, Cream/Hi's board chairman can find a mere human being who can fill that size.

The remarks were flattering, but what the press couldn't include was what I would do next. I wasn't exactly sure. I knew I wanted to pursue a few business ventures with a man named Jim Harding whom I had known for several years.

I first met Harding back in 1945 when I arrived in Los Angeles from Milwaukee. One of my odd jobs was in a Hollywood hospital kitchen as a pot washer. Harding was an assistant cook. He was only eighteen and had recently arrived from Memphis. We became friends and kept in contact occasionally through the years. While my career turned to the record industry, he stayed in the food business. Jim joined the army and became a cook. After he was discharged, he returned to Los

Angeles and opened a little barbeque eatery called Mr. Jim's. By the late 1970s, he had four Mr. Jim's restaurants, which became known as having the best barbeque on the West Coast. People would come from posh Beverly Hills to the south side of Los Angeles for Mr. Jim's barbeque.

Our new business venture was to franchise the restaurant, first opening one near UCLA and another near Woodland Hills, California, then go national. However, we decided to hold off on the franchise idea when the country was hit with the worst economic conditions it had seen in forty years. Jim and I also had a joint real estate venture—a thirty-two-unit senior citizen apartment building on Country Club Drive near the Wilshire district of LA, which we held for a few years before selling. My plan, once back in California, was to pursue other business ventures along with continuing Eddie Ray Music Enterprises.

All that changed when I had lunch one day with my old friend Mike Curb. Curb had become lieutenant governor of California by this time.

"Eddie, what about politics? Why don't you get involved in politics?" he urged in his convincing manner. The question captured enough of my interest and curiosity to respond, "Let's talk about it." That was all Curb needed to hear to put his political clout into motion.

Soon afterward, I started having dinner at Curb's house each week for several weeks to meet a member of the "Kitchen Cabinet," the infamous, well-heeled group credited with making Reagan governor of California and later determined to make him president. I listened to the myriad of ideas that came from each member and gained a close-up view of the power of partisan politics.

However, I had no intention of being pushed or pulled by the standard party system. My MO had always been and still was to operate outside the norm, thus APAC was born, my own political machine of thirteen prominent African-Americans who would support Reagan for president. I did this at the consternation of some family and friends and had to spend time mending fences, but lending my support to the Reagan camp ended up opening doors in some remarkable ways.

I was very careful who I chose for APAC, one member being Attorney Michael Frisby, who did the legal paperwork to officially set up the group. Another was my good friend Harold Cormier, who owned a printing company and did all the printing for the organization. Also included were professional, personal friends who represented the medical, educational, business, political and sports/entertainment interests.

One of APAC's first political moves was to take out a full-page ad in the Los Angeles *Sentinel* for the Reagan/Bush campaign. We noted that Reagan, as governor, had appointed quite a few African-Americans to key executive positions and committees in his administration in California. The ad created the buzz we wanted. *Who in the world is this APAC?* people wondered, especially the county and state Republican committees. No one in California politics had heard of me or the people with me. We then started to hold luncheons and discuss different policies with noted political and community leaders of both political parties. Then in a gutsy move, we opened a Reagan/Bush headquarters on Western Avenue in the heart of the black community, where people would walk by and give us the finger—but the negative reaction created only more publicity.

APAC was on such a roll that we started getting calls from other Republican political candidates wanting our support. My response was always a cool, "Well, you'll have to come talk to us and we'll think about it. We haven't supported anyone except Reagan." Or we'd get a call from someone wanting to join. Again, I'd put on an elitist air and respond, "Actually, we're not taking any memberships right now." People didn't realize that APAC was primarily PR—perhaps smoke and mirrors, but it worked.

One day a call came in that caught my attention. I was being appointed by Mike Curb to go to the California State Republican Convention in Palm Springs as a Republican California state delegate. This later led to me being named a delegate to the Republican National Convention in Detroit in 1980.

I had always been fascinated by the big national conventions when, as a youngster, I'd listen to them on the radio and wonder what it would be like to attend as a delegate. Now in such an unusual turn of life's events, I was about to find out.

Three 747s flew the California delegation to Detroit that July where the 1980 Republican National Convention was being held at the Joe Louis Arena. My plane held many of the "Kitchen Cabinet" members along with Reagan's daughter Maureen. We all stayed at the Renaissance Hotel, at the time the world's tallest hotel. I was on the floor just below Reagan.

What a most memorable experience—there I was in this magnificent hotel with the next president of the United States, while other state delegations were somewhere in less-glamorous accommodations in Detroit. It was a great feeling to be with a soon-to-be winner, especially when you felt you had played an important role in his victory.

Among the hundreds of attendees, African Americans were a rarity, so much so that I attracted media attention. An interview with me made the six o'clock news back in Los Angeles.

Prior to the convention, I became cochairman of the California Black Republicans for Reagan/Bush, a position that put me directly on Reagan's radar. On one occasion, I'd spent the day with him, attending different functions on the campaign trail. With my close friend Mike Curb as acting California governor and Reagan as the Republican's presidential choice, I was sandwiched between two of the most powerful men in the country.

Then in June of 1981, following Reagan's presidential win over incumbent Jimmy Carter, I received a call from Curb. He informed me that there would be a vacancy on the US Copyright Royalty Tribunal because one of President Carter's appointees was resigning and President Reagan requested Curb's advice for his replacement because of Curb's knowledge of the music industry.

Curb asked me who I would recommend for the position. After a long conversation, he said, "Eddie, what about you?" He continued, "You said that you and Jim had put a temporary hold on your restaurant franchise venture and the unexpired term on the tribunal is only for a year and a half. By the end of the term, business may have improved and you can continue with your plans."

Shortly after our conversation, I called Curb and told him to submit my name to the president for the position. A few months later, President Reagan announced his intention to nominate me as a US Commissioner of the Copyright Royalty Tribunal, headquartered in Washington, DC.

The Copyright Royalty Tribunal, or CRT, as it was called, was created by Congress in 1978 under Jimmy Carter to be an independent agency that would set royalty fees and administer certain mandatory copyright license rates for music, sports, radio, TV, and cable entertainment programs. For instance the CRT was in charge of mechanical license rates for the making and distribution of records; rates and royalty fees for music in jukeboxes; and copyright rates for the retransmission of certain broadcast signals by cable companies and satellite carriers. Basically the tribunal's goal was to make sure music copyright owners were compensated for music used over the airwaves and cable, and if the copyright owner could not be located, the royalty fees still had to be paid into a fund set up by the tribunal and later distributed by the CRT to the copyright owners once located.

As with any political appointment, mine was not without opposition. It wasn't because I would be a Republican coming onto the Democrat-dominated tribunal or because I was African American. The opposition came from the National Music Publishers Association. At the time of my appointment, animosity existed between record companies and music publishers—almost like the Hatfields and McCoys. The publishers who held copyrights wanted more money from record people, and the record people wanted to pay less in royalties.

The National Music Publishers Association opposed my appointment because they viewed me as a "record man." They were not aware of my music publishing background, my owning both ASCAP and BMI publishing companies through Eddie Ray Music Enterprises. Most were unaware—but ironically, not all. As head of the music publishing giant ATV, my friend Sam Trust, one of my life's long, strong, colorful threads, happened to be on the association's board during this time. He spoke up on my behalf along with Wesley Rose of Acuff-Rose Music Publishing in Nashville.

The two of them changed the tenor of the group, which in turn dropped its opposition. My appointment was approved by the Senate, and before I knew it, I was moving to Washington, DC.

The tribunal was located in a Federal Building at Twentieth and L Streets NW, only a few blocks from the White House. I lived in Falls Church, Virginia, a beautiful, quiet little town about seven miles from the District.

I moved to Washington alone, but wouldn't leave that way.

CHAPTER TWENTY-ONE

ANOTHER SEVEN YEARS

U pon fulfilling the year-and-a half term of the retiring commissioner, the president reappointed me to a full seven-year term on the tribunal. So I continued to dig my teeth into the various issues with which the commissioners were grappling. The tribunal was responsible for adjusting certain compulsory statutory royalty rates that those who wanted to use copyrighted music had to pay copyright owners. When these rates were raised for the first time since 1908 from two cents, to five cents, to seven cents, and then to nine cents, it meant literally billions of dollars flowed through the entertainment industry.

That of course brought many claimants before the tribunal. In many cases our final determinations in rate adjustment or royalty distribution hearings were appealed to the Second Federal Circuit Court in Washington, DC. In fact, one case went all the way to the Supreme Court, but in each situation the court rejected the appeals and upheld our determination.

Not only did cable, record company, and satellite executives rail us because of our decisions, but even evangelists, referred to as "religious claimants," joined the critics' bandwagon. They said they should have received a larger share of the royalty pool because their programs were the most valuable because they "save souls" on the air. They went so far as to accuse us of being against religion—downright heathens. Some of the situations were almost comical.

Then groups such as motion picture and sports representatives had a different argument. They claimed that the popularity of their programs were responsible for most of the cable viewers. Therefore they should receive a larger percentage of the fees flowing into the US Treasury coffers. ASCAP and BMI also had their hand out because of music in movies, situation comedies, and every type of cable program. I had just about seen and heard it all during my eight years on the CRT, four of which I served as chair.

I wasn't surprised by the criticism the tribunal received. It can be expected toward any governmental agency proposing change. What did take me aback a bit was encountering opposition from within.

Marianne Mele Hall was an ambitious young lady appointed to the tribunal by President Reagan to fill an unexpired term of a retiring commissioner. Once she settled in, Mele Hall evidently did not want me or a Cuban-American colleague on the commission and attempted to acquire the chairmanship to have more power on the tribunal.

Her tactic to have us removed was to romance the Hill to get Congress to change laws governing tribunal appointments. She pushed that members should be attorneys only. Since my Hispanic colleague and I were the only two non attorneys on the CRT at the time, she envisioned our fate being sealed. But as fate would have it, her efforts ended up being her own undoing.

While Mele Hall garnered attention for her campaign to change the appointment laws, she never failed to mention, actually bragged on the fact, that she had coauthored a book. She found a way to work this accomplishment into the conversation of every meeting, dinner, or interview—that's until a reporter for one interview secured a copy of the book, entitled *Foundations of Sand*, and read it.

The book contained disparaging remarks about African Americans, suggesting they were genetically inferior to Caucasians. According to the book, African American men in US ghettos "still hold to their African traditions...They insist on preserving their jungle freedoms, their women, their avoidance of personal responsibility, and their abhorrence of the work ethic."

When phrases from the book came to light in the media and critics questioned Mele Hall, she quickly backpedaled, saying she didn't coauthor the book, only edited it, and claimed as an editor, "you don't need to understand what you're reading." However, despite her efforts to distance herself from the book, it was too late. The damage had been done to her character, and she was forced to resign from the tribunal.

I watched the events unfold bemused. My only thought was that Mele Hall was a neophyte when it came to Washington politics. I kept my distance from the firestorm surrounding her. My Copyright Royalty Tribunal Confidential Assistant Christy Rodriguez recalls that controversial time:

> There were a few difficult moments that Eddie handled with grace and confident composure—the condescending reference to him as a "roadie for a rock band" by a member of Congress during the Marianne Mele Hall flap, and his delicate and capable handling of [Mele Hall], his fellow Reagan appointee, an admitted collaborator on a book that espoused a genetic inferiority of blacks and Latinos. Those were hard and insulting times that called for vision and balance to ensure a just and appropriate outcome. Eddie succeeded with both—an apology from the congressman and the timely departure of Ms. Mele Hall.

Sometimes the wisest course of action is to allow certain situations to run their course—water seeks its own level.

Although the day-to-day CRT duties were quite demanding, especially when I became chair of the commission, the position didn't consume all of my attention. I made time for the Washington social scene, which I admittedly enjoyed. Invitations to lunches, banquets, and receptions poured in, and I attended when I could. I became a Republican Eagle, an exclusive high-donor contributor to the Republican National Committee, and a member of the Capitol Hill Club, a prestigious, private Republican club. Both positions gave me access to the president, his cabinet members, and important Republican congressmen.

The federal building at Twentieth and L Streets NW, which housed my CRT office, was also home to a number of other agencies, one of which was the Foreign Claims Settlement Commission (FCSC), an agency of the Justice Department.

Leaving the office late one day, on my way to a social engagement, I encountered a lovely lady at the elevator. I asked her for directions to the event, which she readily provided. A few weeks later, I encountered her again outside the building.

In an effort to strike up a conversation, I ventured, "You must know something about this building that I don't. I never see you in the elevator. How do you get downstairs?"

"Walking down the stairs is healthier for you," she briefly responded.

We didn't introduce ourselves, but the next day I decided to find out who she was. I went to one of my colleagues at the CRT, Barbara Gray, and described the woman I had twice run into.

"She's pretty, rather small, and always has a smile and a wonderful personality."

"You must be talking about Jeanette Matthews," Ms. Gray responded. I later asked more questions and found out Jeanette worked for the Foreign Claims Settlement Commission on the same floor as the CRT. With more questioning I led up to whether Ms. Matthews was married and if Barbara would give me her phone number.

As Jeanette recalls today, "Barbara came to my office and said, 'Eddie Ray met a young lady who works in the building, and after describing her to a T, I knew it was you.' Afterward he asked Barbara if she had my phone number because he wanted to invite me to lunch. She consulted with me, and I said she could give him the number. My first impression of Eddie was that he was new to the city and just wanted a female companion only to get through his supposedly short stay and that he was not looking for a serious relationship. Immediately my guard went up, but not for long because he showered me with lunches, trips, and gifts."

Jeanette and I began an extended courtship that lasted some ten years. We were married in 1991. She's right that when we first met, I wasn't planning to stay in Washington long—only a year and a half to finish the first CRT appointment. Even with my reappointment, I was eventually headed back to California where Jeanette had no intentions of going, wanting to stay close to her family in Washington. So year in and year out, we just enjoyed lunches, going to events, and taking trips, not sure where our relationship would end up.

By 1989 my term with the tribunal was coming to an end. The work of the group had changed so much by then that I knew it was only a matter of time before the tribunal was "sunsetted." The parties that once came before us with disputes began reaching settlements on their own. Commissioners who retired or left were not being replaced, and by the late '80s we were down to three commissioners. Also by that time, the work of the commission had little involvement in rate setting but was primarily involved in distribution settlements. However, before I left the CRT, with the support of fellow commissioner Katherine Ortega, I was able to bring about a major change.

In the early years of the Copyright Royalty Tribunal's existence, the government had been footing the bill, yet most of the service we rendered in our royalty distribution hearings was on behalf of public broadcast, motion picture, sports, and music publishing companies. Very little time was spent in rate adjustment hearings because those determinations were usually for multiple years. I thought, *Why shouldn't these companies pick up the tab instead of taxpayers?* After a significant amount of political haranguing, my proposal was accepted, and by the time of my departure, 90 percent of the cost of the CRT was being paid by the claimants.

A couple years after I left, the tribunal was dissolved, but years later the role came back under the government's copyright office, primarily resolving Internet copyright rates and distribution disputes.

On September 29, 1989, to my surprise, representatives of copyright owners and users who had appeared before the tribunal—several who once considered us an adversary—had a huge going-away dinner party for me to genuinely wish me well. I understand this was the first and only time such a tribute was paid to a commissioner.

Also to my surprise, going back to California wasn't in the cards. The next day, I was off to Texas.

CHAPTER TWENTY-TWO

A REMARKABLE JOURNEY

I will always be amazed at how individuals have entered my life, retreated, and later resurfaced in a significant way. That's why I can only picture a tapestry as I think of them, interlaced threads that are sometimes visible on the front surface adding color and texture to a unique design and then woven to the underside, still an important part of the picture but not visible. Then suddenly, unexpectedly they resurface, at just the right moment to once again add to the work of art. That was the case with my Texas connection, the late renowned saxophonist Larry "T-Byrd" Gordon, whom I had first encountered while at Cream/Hi Records in Memphis.

Not long before I was to bid farewell to Washington and the Copyright Royalty Tribunal, the phone rang. It was Gordon. We hadn't talked for quite some time, so he first brought me up to date on his activities. He had received his PhD, was still teaching at a junior college in Texas, and was playing local gigs throughout Dallas. Gordon's wife, Carrie, was a member of the Dallas Zoning Commission, and this is where the conversation took a turn.

T-Byrd and Carrie explained that a revitalization project was about to get underway in the community of Las Colinas, a twelve-thousand-acre stretch between Dallas and Fort Worth. Part of the plan was to create an entertainment district as one of the highlights.

"We want you to be a consultant to our new music publishing/recording company that we're planning to locate in Las Colinas," T-Byrd said.

The person developing the area was billionaire real estate mogul Trammell Crow, called one of America's largest landlords. He once had interests in nearly three hundred million square feet of developed real estate, comprising eight thousand properties in more than one hundred cities. In fact, I lived in one of his apartment complexes in Alexandria, Virginia, and had met him through Mike Curb some years prior when I was involved in Reagan's presidential campaign. With Crow bankrolling the Las Colinas project, I knew it was worth investigating.

Soon after talking with the Gordons, I flew to Texas to discuss the consultant agreement with them and to meet with the group working on the Las Colinas project. Already in the area was a production studio where portions of the *Dallas* TV show were taped. Sony Records also had set up a distribution center in Las Colinas, so adding more entertainment entities seemed a natural progression. I signed a two-year contract to be a consultant on the Gordons' commercial music production company project, and on September 30, 1989, the day after my CRT farewell, I was off to Dallas. I moved to Mesquite,

Texas, and lived, once again, in a Trammell Crow apartment community.

I had hoped Jeanette would be able to join me soon. Maybe the right job would pry her loose from Washington. But we were unable to find a comparable position for her and she was too far from retirement, so we began a long-distance courtship.

After much consideration, the Gordons and I decided not to locate their new music company in Las Colinas but elsewhere in the South Dallas area. As part of my consultant responsibilities, I advised and supervised the creation of their ASCAP and BMI Music Publishing Company; the construction of a state-of-the-art recording studio; and the development of new and more successful methods to book and promote the public performances of Gordon's band. But my interest was always focused on T-Byrd's exceptional talent and how to establish him as a major entertainment star. His band, The Larry T-Byrd Gordon Review, was too good to perform for a few hundred dollars a night at small local clubs.

"T-Byrd, you need to do corporate affairs, the country club set," I urged. Eventually through the help of people like then Dallas City Manager Jim Reid, and other influential political and business people I met, in no time T-Byrd's group became known as the "high-society band," doing just about every major event throughout Texas. It performed at events for people like billionaire Ross Perot and major national corporations located in Texas. His band went from a few hundred dollars to several thousand dollars per appearance.

One of his gigs was at a popular, upscale restaurant in Texas. The restaurant owner's mother had done some acting with Grace Kelly and was also a close friend of the star, who lived in Monte Carlo. Although the mother never became a big star, she maintained contact with Kelly and later with Prince

Rainier after Kelly's death. Through them, Gordon was invited to perform at the famed Monte-Carlo yacht races. After that first time, he was invited back for nine straight years. One year a woman saw his band and brought the whole group, including me, to East Berlin for her husband's birthday party. We stayed, literally, in an unbelievable castle, each of us enjoying a private suite. We were treated like rock stars in East Berlin, complete with body guards.

Being instrumental in Gordon landing that kind of clientele was most rewarding for me as it took me back to the heydays of building the careers of new stars at Imperial, Capitol, and MGM. T-Byrd, Carrie, Jeanette, and I developed a strong friendship through the years. His sudden death was a great personal loss to me. At his funeral, over fifteen hundred people celebrated his life, including many of his former college students and music fans. I'm honored to be the godfather to their son, Larry Gordon II. Fondly known as "Lil Larry," he's a rising star in his own right as a singer, songwriter, and record producer. Not long ago I was instrumental in getting him signed to the Curb/Warner Record Group in Nashville.

My days in Texas as a consultant with the Gordons were unexpectedly cut short, right in the midst of my two-year contract. It was on a routine visit to my physician back in Washington, DC, that the words "clogged arteries" hung over me like a thick fog as medical procedures were discussed. I ended my contract and moved back to the Washington area. The best part of this move was that Jeanette and I could be together again. Knowing that I would stay put for awhile, we decided not to squander any more time and married in the spring of

1991. Then, that fall, I had triple bypass surgery after several balloon angioplasties did not yield the desired results.

The surgery meant I had to pull in the reigns, to slow way down, to finally retire, or so I thought. It gave me time to reflect, to write, and to focus on my beautiful wife. As it always happened, however, a few years later, the phone rang and it was Mike Curb with an offer.

"Tell me about the commercial music school you started in Memphis," Curb inquired. After discussing in detail the establishment and operation of my Memphis commercial music school, Curb went on to explain that he was interested in starting a similar school in Nashville and wanted me to participate in it with him. Without listening to additional details of what he had in mind, I turned him down, describing first my recent health challenges and then those of Jeanette. I had no idea that his school would become so huge, primarily because of the generous monetary gifts of the Mike Curb Family Foundation.

Today the Mike Curb Family Foundation has a list of philanthropic endeavors a mile long, many supporting music education. There's the Mike Curb College of Entertainment and Music Business, the largest college at Belmont University in Nashville. In fact, Belmont's Curb Event Center made the news when it hosted the historic presidential debate between then candidates Barack Obama and John McCain in 2008. There's also The Mike Curb College of Art, Media, and Communication, one of the largest colleges at California State University and The Curb College of Arts, Music, and Science at Daytona State College. And Rhodes College in Memphis has The Mike Curb Institute for Music. The foundation has endowments at institutions all over the country. I sometimes wonder what my life would have been like in these later years had I accepted his offer. What I don't wonder about is how Curb became so successful. I knew he would be. I spotted it back in the early 1960s when he first came to my office. He has never forgotten that day nor have I.

I didn't hear from Mike Curb for a number of years after that—not until 2007 when he called again.

"Eddie, why isn't there a music hall of fame in North Carolina?" An intriguing question.

This time I accepted Curb's offer on this new venture, and in less than two years the permanent home of the North Carolina Music Hall of Fame opened in downtown Kannapolis, NC, with me as vice chairman and operations director. Numerous artifacts for the museum had already been collected over the years by various individuals hoping for a museum one day.

My move to North Carolina meant a commuter marriage for me and Jeanette, but now with her retired, she could spend long stretches of time with me while maintaining our primary residence in the Washington area.

Kannapolis was selected for the museum's location because of Curb's long tie with the town through his interests in NASCAR and his Curb Motor Sports and Music Museum there. He has an even longer tie with David H. Murdock, owner of Dole Foods. The food magnate, who owns quite a bit of real estate in Kannapolis, had recently built a 1.5-billion-dollar biotechnology and nutrition research campus in downtown. The new Music Hall of Fame, within walking distance of the research campus, would add to the area's attractions. Curb and Murdock had been business colleagues and longtime friends stemming from Curb's political activity in California in the '70s.

The plaque at the entrance to the North Carolina Music Hall of Fame reads:

This Building Restored
By The Mike Curb Family Foundation
In Honor Of
Edward "Eddie" Ray
2008

Trying to explain the plaque to museum visitors and my connection with Mike Curb is like trying to explain why the sky is blue—it's just one of those always-has-been-always-will-be blessings for both of us.

And now, on this October 3 night at the David H. Murdock Core Laboratory, the pinnacle of the North Carolina Research Campus, with its marbled floors and gold elevators, I approach the microphone. I have just heard my friend Mike Curb introduce me, saying that I could cross all genres of music, that I started a school of commercial music, and that I had been appointed by the president of the United States and confirmed by the Senate as a commissioner to the US Copyright Royalty Tribunal. He mentioned my grandfather who was once a slave, and called me one of the great Americans of all time.

"I never thought I would have this opportunity," I say, humbly accepting the North Carolina Music Hall of Fame inductee award. I first thank Jeanette for her patience and support and then take the audience back to the mid-1940s, thanking Leo and Eddie Mesner for giving me my first education in the music business.

Both Larry "T-Byrd" Gordon and his son "Lil Larry" are there to serenade me, amidst the host of family and friends. And on this special night, as I look back on all the events, the people, the opportunities that brought me to this point, that make up my life's tapestry, the only word that comes to my mind is *remarkable*.

Epilogue

Eddie Ray is currently the vice chairman and operations director of the North Carolina Music Hall of Fame, located at 109 West A Street in Kannapolis, North Carolina. The popular tourist attraction features memorabilia from many famous recording artists as well as others who have made a significant contribution to the music world. As of this writing, those inducted include:

Chairmen of the Board	Ben E. King
Kay Kyser	Earl Scruggs
Bill Griffin	Roberta Flack
Loonis McGlohon	Randy Travis
Victoria Livengood	George Clinton
Billy Scott	Nina Simone
Charlie Daniels	Johnny Bristol
Ronnie Milsap	James Taylor

Max Roach

Clyde McPhatter

Thelonious Monk

Kate Smith

The Five Royales

Johnny Grant

Mike Curb

Wilbert Harrison

Eddie Ray

John Coltrane

Maurice Williams

Andy Griffith

Donna Fargo

Arthur Smith

George Hamilton IV

Doc Watson

Curly Seckler

Dr. Billy Taylor

Shirley Caesar

Don Gibson

Les Brown

William Oliver Swofford

Don Schlitz

Clyde Moody

Maceo Parker

Billy Crash Craddock

Billy Edd Wheeler

Tori Amos

Shirley Austin Reeves & Doris

Kenner Jackson

Jodeci

Nantucket

Stonewall Jackson

Lou Donaldson

J. E. Mainer

Fred Foster

Michael English

Ben Folds

Anthony Dean Griffey

John D. Loudermilk

Find out more at www.northcarolinamusichalloffame.org

About the Coauthor

Barbara Jackson Hall is a former TV news reporter, talk show host, and health magazine editor who interviewed dozens of personalities in her twenty-year career in the communications industry. Currently, she is director of the Small Business Center at Rowan-Cabarrus Community College in North Carolina, where she helps individuals fulfill their dream of business ownership. Her office is located in Kannapolis, North Carolina, a few blocks from the North Carolina Music Hall of Fame where she first met Eddie Ray at the grand opening in 2009. After hearing a bit of his story, she was compelled to help him recount his life in a book to preserve a slice of African-American history.